TURN
PHRASE

Radical Theology from A to Z

Don Cupitt

scm press

For
the Master and Fellows
of Emmanuel College, Cambridge

© Don Cupitt 2011

Published in 2011 by SCM Press
Editorial office
13–17 Long Lane,
London, EC1A 9PN, UK

SCM Press is an imprint of Hymns Ancient & Modern Ltd
(a registered charity)
13A Hellesdon Park Road
Norwich NR6 5DR, UK
www.scmpress.co.uk

British Library Cataloguing in Publication data

A catalogue record for this book is available
from the British Library

978-0-334-04419-2

Originated by the Manila Typesetting Company
Printed and bound by
CPI Antony Rowe, Chippenham, Wiltshire

Contents

G   Ghostly titles; Globalization;
Glory; God; God, a 'leading' idea;
'God is a secular humanist';
The Highest Good, the Summum Bonum;
Good show!; Grand Narrative, great Story

H   Heresy, heretic; Heterologous
thinking; Heteronomy; Etty Hillesum;
Humanism; The Human Lifeworld;
Human realism; Humanitarian ethics

I   Identity; Impossible Loves;
Inside out; Internalization;
'The Interpretative Plasticity
of the World'

J   The Jesus of History and
the Christ of Faith

K   Kingdom-religion, Kingdom theology

L   Landscape Art, Eastern and
Western; Language is only about
itself, Language is much cleverer
than the people who speak it, Language
speaks us, Let language do the talking;
The Leap of Reason; Life, The Religion
of Ordinary Life; Life's a Package Deal;
We live along the wires, etc.; Lost in the
objectivity of world-love; Lucifer

M   Make out, make, believe, make sense,
making the most of It; Meaning,
mean-ing; Mediated and immediate
religion; Metaphysical evil; Misandry,
misotheism; 'Your mind is in front of
your face'; Mind, 'minding';
Our M/Other; Mysticism: 'Mysticism is
not a kind of experience; it is a kind of
transgressive writing'

The Books

Introduction

Called upon by her wrathful mistress to account for her sudden and unannounced production of a baby, the Victorian maidservant couldn't do any better than offer a plea in mitigation: 'It's only a *little* one, Ma'am.'

I'm in an equally embarrassing position. At the beginning of 2011 I had just published what was touted as my forty-seventh and last book. The paper Cupitt who has ruled my life for about 45 years had all been put into boxes and was in process of being removed to a Library, where he would be shut up, silent, and above all, *a long way from me*. All seemed set fair. But then I found I was pregnant yet again, and could have no rest until I had begun writing. At my age.

My excuse is like the young maid's. It's not a *real* book. It's what Derrida, being French, called an *Hors d'œuvre*, outside the main body of work. Not really a *new* book, but a dictionary of my ideas that may help, if not to excuse, then at least to *explain* me, and also may serve as a dictionary or workbook in modern religious thought. I have been very piqued this past few years by the number of people who complain that my books are hopelessly obscure, irrelevant, name-dropping, too philosophical, too radical, and so on. I've knocked myself out for decades, trying to copy the great literary philosophers who wrote very short and clear books – Plato, Descartes, Nietzsche. I've produced large numbers of short summaries, along the lines of Buddhism's Four Noble Truths, Three Jewels and Eightfold Path. I've tried fancy literary techniques in trying to communicate the way my ideas hang together. And it's not gone at all well. Reviewers read my books apparently without noticing anything at all of what I am trying to say.

Why does this happen? In 1900 Adolf Harnack could summarize his radical theology in a phrase – 'The Fatherhood of God and the brotherhood of Man' – and had no problem. In 1963 John Robinson's radical theology reached people not through one but through several short phrases, but still he was easily able to reach a wide public. He did well enough to destroy his own career: he was very lucky to do as well as that. But today the problems (as Robinson himself foresaw) are far worse. It is not possible to see any future for religion except after a major intellectual transformation, *far* greater in scale than either the one that occurred at the Reformation in sixteenth-century Europe, or the one envisaged by nineteenth-century liberal theology after F. D. E. Schleiermacher. If you want real religion now, you will have to pay a very high price for it. You need a complete mental valeting.

Especially since the Second World War, the pace of cultural change has accelerated dramatically. All the world's ancient religious and cultural traditions are in acute crisis. It looks as if most of them can survive only as 'heritage' – tourist attractions – or by selling out to militant ethno-nationalist identity-politics. People like to wear a badge of identity that makes clear whose side they are on, and they increasingly use religion for just that purpose. I utterly abhor this gross debasement of religion, but what's the alternative? There seems currently to be no serious religion, producing good-quality writing, anywhere in the world. What's happening? In the past I have often cited the huge growth and rapid spread of modern critical thinking and critically tested knowledge, and especially the application of the critical style of thinking to the scriptures, the doctrines and the histories of the major faith-traditions. But there's more to it than that. In the Axial Age, when systematic thinking about the world, about the human condition, and about the good life first began, religious and philosophical thinking were not clearly distinguished from each other. All our great religious systems grew up with a lot of philosophy built around them and with many deep philosophical assumptions buried inside them. So many, that without a lot of history-of-philosophy you simply cannot understand today what God was once supposed to be and what so-called 'belief in God' involved. If you doubt this, try checking out the standard list of the old God's 'metaphysical attributes' and the way they all connected together. Next, I challenge you to name the last standard textbook about God – Jewish or Christian or Muslim – in which the whole traditional doctrine of God is confidently spelt out as something that all believers know and accept. When was it, and what was its title? I know you don't know. In fact the huge development of modern knowledge and of philosophy has changed our world-view so much that it has exposed all the old metaphysical assumptions – and we realize that we don't think like that any more, and simply *cannot* think like that any more. But that means that we no longer have the vocabulary in which we can state clearly what God is, or was once, supposed to be.

In short, the whole architecture of 'traditional' religious belief is *philosophically* ruined, and we cannot begin to do religious thinking again until we have cleared away mountains of rubble. And the job is *philosophical*. One cannot just abridge the Creed: one has to undergo a major intellectual revolution. And I as much as anyone can testify that it is traumatic.

In my books, I tried to write *both* for a 'trade' or general audience *and* at top level, because I have always thought that that is how philosophy began and how it should be written – *especially* the 'human' kind of philosophy that deals with religion, art, morality and politics. I tried to keep technical terms to the minimum, and instead aimed to challenge the reader by inventing fresh and startling slogans. For example, I tried to break people out of the usual talk about 'mind and body' by producing slogans like 'Your mind is in front of your face', and 'We live along the wires, and are ourselves in our communicative relations with other people', and 'Your interpretation of me is probably just as good as my interpretation of me', and, even more provocative: 'I have no evidence about me that isn't in principle equally available to you'. The point of writing in this way is to try to change your thinking, and get you out of the old metaphysics of substance that has people thinking that a thing called 'a mind' is in their heads, like the pilot in a plane's cockpit. And at least I don't lecture you about 'externalism'.

I love systematics, but most people don't like philosophical systems, so in this dictionary of words and ideas and phrases I have included a number of crosslinks in boldface type. The idea is that you'll keep this book by your bed and will read one entry, which will lead you to another, and so on until you have wandered through a good deal of my world. Use the book often enough in this way, and you will in the end painlessly absorb the system. I hope. I maintain that almost any radical theology, or attempt to renew religious thought today, must run pretty close to what I present here, so the book is by no means just about me, and you might in fact want to get out some paper and start writing some of your own.

This guide to my world and workbook was written to the ghostly title, *The Devil's Dictionary*. The American journalist (and rather Mark-Twain-like figure) Ambrose Bierce (1842–1914?) published *A Cynic's Wordbook* in 1906, and then changed its title in 1911 to *The Devil's Dictionary*. The title suits me, because I still occasionally meet people who really think I *am* the Devil. They truly *shudder* when they hear my name. The reason for this is that conservative religious belief is impressed upon people with very great violence, and is only given up with acute pain and with the utmost reluctance. Often one has a 'breakdown'. Society is very protective of its traditions, which have attached to them very effective 'blocks to falsifiability'. If I frighten people so much that they think I'm the Devil, it must be because they are terrified that I present a real danger to them.

Here you will find no Index, because it *is* an index, and there are very few big names or learned references. In *Above Us Only Sky* I tried to present myself in 27 slogans, not mentioning that many of them were actually quotes from Leo Tolstoy, because that would have killed them. Academia kills ideas, stuffs them, labels them, and mounts them in its imaginary museum. You don't want that. So I hope in this book to be entertaining, to get under your guard, and painlessly to smuggle something of my system into yours. *Life Lines* (1986) was my best previous attempt to write an interactive book in which the reader would find her or his own personal journey already mapped. It worked for a few readers, and in the next few years three autobiographies stole my title.

If you notice any important omissions, please let me know, and if I am able to do so, I will incorporate them in any reprint that may be called for. Perhaps, if you do annotate your copy of this book, you or your heirs may one day care to put your annotated copy into my archive at Hawarden? Just for a bit of reader-response.

Don Cupitt
Cambridge, 2011

A

'Above us only sky'. A line from John Lennon's 1973 song, 'Imagine', nowadays to be seen posted high up at John Lennon International Airport, Liverpool, UK. Compare the young Karl Marx: 'Man is the highest being for man'. I used the phrase as the title of a 2008 book.

Actus Purus (pure act). Aristotle distinguished actuality from potentiality. A thing may be actual in some respects, while in other respects its potentialities are as yet unrealized. In the classical Christian doctrine of God, God is said to be pure act because, being perfect and changeless, he cannot have *any* unfulfilled potentialities. He is **all out**, always. But a being that is eternally all out is **'solar'**, like the Sun. It *is* its own burning, its own self-outing, its own perpetually **dying life**. See also **Death of God**.

Aestheticism. In my use, *not* just the late nineteenth-century doctrine of 'Art for art's sake', associated with Beerbohm, Wilde, Beardsley and *The Yellow Book*, but a wider doctrine which makes aesthetics, the philosophy of art, central to our understanding of ourselves and **our world**. Experience gives us only chaotic raw data: we use general symbols – words, numbers, pictures, etc. – to capture, order and interpret our experience, our relations with each other and ourselves. So **our world**, the only world we have, may be described as 'our communal, partly botched work of folk art'. We together are making and remaking it all the time.

Thinking along these lines is to be found not only in Nietzsche but also in Ernst Cassirer (1874–1945), whose major work is *The Philosophy of Symbolic Forms* (1923–9, Eng. trans. 1953–7). He turned Kant's philosophy in a constructivist direction – 'we are the world-builders' – and described man as 'the symbolic animal'. All human cultural achievements, including the creation of language, mathematics,

1

science, art and religion, may thus come to be seen as human symbolic constructions, and as being all pretty much on a level. None of them *has* to be taken as referring to anything other than itself, just as a word's meaning is given simply in other words.

If we interpret religious thought along these lines, we'll see the typically religious act not as a withdrawal into passivity and submission to Almighty Power, but as energetic creative activity. Asked whether he believed in God, Henri Matisse is said to have replied: 'Yes – when I'm working.' However, it would be a mistake to lay all the emphasis upon a few exceptionally creative individuals. In more recent French philosophy culture is seen as a great system of signs in motion, a continuous process of symbolic exchange to which each of us makes some contribution. The current state of the world, current values and the current state of knowledge in every subject all hang suspended within a slowly shifting public consensus. Nothing is 'absolute' or anchored; everything heaves and rolls like the sea, and we with it.

In traditional Western religious thought the *consensus fidelium* (the agreement of the faithful) was an important criterion of truth ('the Vincentian canon'). A form of that idea has returned in **postmodern** philosophy. Truth is just 'the current state of the argument'.

All out. See **Actus Purus,** above. To be all out is to express oneself fully and uninhibitedly, to be open, candid, and truthful – to be **solar.** At some point, perhaps around the time of Nietzsche and Oscar Wilde, modern people began to turn away from the old spirituality of hidden inwardness – concealment of the truth about oneself – and began instead to insist upon 'coming out'. A religious imperative requires of us, not introversion, but extraversion. We need to come out of the closet and be our true selves in public. We should *burn*. Note here the rise of terms like **expressionism, expressivism** and **emotivism.**

In the so-called 'Sermon on the Mount', the two spiritualities are presented side by side. In Matthew 6.1–21, Jesus teaches the Church-spirituality of hiddenness, and even secretiveness. But in other passages, much closer to the thought of the original Jesus, he teaches the all out, solar way uncompromisingly: see for example Matthew 5.13–16; 6.25–34. It is his greatest originality. He preached the final world, and above all, taught its **solar** ethic. See also **coming out, spirituality**.

'All this is all there is'. A phrase I often use to make the point that the ordinary human lifeworld, the world that is given us in the language we use and hear used every day, is the only world. **This is it.** We should give up all ideas that we can hope for a radically better world in the far future or in Heaven after death. Nor is there a distinct 'real' world underlying the world as it appears to us. No, this transitory human world we build is all there is, and all we'll ever know.

Two consequences follow. First, this world is the *last* world we'll ever know. But the traditional Church-Christianity that began to develop around the year 50 under the leadership of James, Peter and Paul is entirely based on the assumption that the coming of the last world, the 'Kingdom of God' preached by Jesus, has been delayed. The Church is a disciplinary structure, an 'army' that marshals the faithful and keeps them vigilant, looking out for the Lord's return. The Church, on this account, is situated in the *penultimate* world.

Now, the end of all forms of supernatural and metaphysical belief in a Better World to Come forces a change of dispensation. We're not in the Years of Grace any longer. We are already in the last world and must therefore work out a new '**Kingdom' religion** and ethics which lives this life to the full while we have it. I mark this big change of dispensation by using the phrase '**Classical Christianity is now our Old Testament**' – that is, the change of dispensation we are now undergoing is about as big as the last one, which was the change from BC to AD.

3

Analogy is a Greek word equivalent to the Latin words *ratio* or *proportio*. It is much used in the philosophy of religion in trying to explain how human language can be employed to speak meaningfully about God.

Already in the prophet Isaiah it is acknowledged that God is strictly incomparable, and Socrates makes a similar point in the parable of the Cave in Plato's *Republic*. We cannot say anything about God or about the heavenly world which is 'literally' or 'univocally' true. God is too different, as one might say.

A classic but very crude attempt to justify talk of God relies on an old maxim about causality: as a son tends to look like his father, so effects tend to resemble their causes. So there must be in God their creator something analogous to our human wisdom, goodness, fatherhood, etc., for after all, we do meaningfully call a jacket 'warm' if it causes the person who wears it to feel warm. And so on. But I needn't waste time on this feeble argument. It recalls the fact that in animated cartoons, when a flatiron falls on Tom Cat's head, it leaves his head *looking like* a flatiron. The effect is thought to resemble its cause.

More seriously, it is claimed that there is an analogy between (say) divine wisdom and human wisdom, in that God is wise in God's way and a man may be wise in a human way. But this tells us nothing unless we know how God's kind of being differs from our human kind of being. And we don't. They differ *infinitely*, by definition. So the problem of analogy has never been solved, and in the great tradition that lasted till about the year 1200, the standard move was to put the 'Negative Way' first: the only true statements we can make about God are negations such as 'God is not-p'. Later on, the idea gradually developed that the very concrete human language about God used in the Bible does *not* give us any theoretical or speculative knowledge about God, but rather functions to show us how we should live. It is not informative, but 'regulative'. This classic doctrine was the immediate forerunner of my later explicit **non-realism**, and amongst

Anglicans had passed for (just about) orthodox in the period around 1660–1860. I started from it in my first published writings.

The Answer. From the past we have inherited the belief that because an almighty and all-wise Creator has created all things with us in view, and because he has created us in the image of his own rationality, the world is like a book that we can read, a book that contains, all ready for us, definitive Answers to all our questions – answers just right for *us*, couched in our own vocabulary. **Truth** is out there. Even today, there are still people who see 'research' as being like a classical detective's enquiry – a search for the clues that will help us to solve a cosmic mystery or answer a great riddle. In the thriller genre, there may be a scientist who has discovered a magic Formula of great power, who is being pursued by enemy agents. He must not fall into their hands, or we are lost.

I hold that we should free ourselves from all forms of the belief in a final **Revelation** of the whole Truth. As Wittgenstein puts it crisply: 'Nothing is hidden.' But, if I cannot accept traditional ideas of revelation (unveiling; in Greek, 'apocalypse'), I am bound to pursue my own enquiry by the method of philosophy. Hence my problems. The protestant reformers mostly disapproved of philosophy, teaching that 'faith alone' and 'scripture alone' were all we would ever need. This has left many protestant cultures rather antiphilosophical – especially in the English-speaking world. Hence the often-quoted remark that when people lose orthodox religious faith, they don't believe *nothing*: they'll believe *anything*, because they haven't got philosophical thinking to fall back on.

Anthropomonism, Hominism. The word **anthropomonism** was coined by me as a variant of the term 'Christomonism', often used to describe the theology of Karl Barth. '**Hominism**' – also meaning radical humanism – was coined by the Anglo-American philosopher F. C. S. Schiller. To be brutal, it means: 'You're on your own'. Every human being grows up in a language group, and every living human language carries within it a complete world-picture. Every human being therefore has access to a complete world-picture. But we don't know of any other being who has a (non-human) world-picture or indeed a complete language. Therefore we cannot clearly distinguish **our world** from **the world**. In effect, we-in-our-world are all there is. We're on our own now.

Radical **Humanism** of this kind may be seen as always having been latent within Christianity. Look at any first-millennium image of Christ Almighty, a human being enthroned over the Cosmos. A historical man is bigger than the whole world, because he is the Maker.

Artist. In Church-Christianity the believer was spoken of as a soldier, *miles Christi*, who joins a great institution which finds him a place and tells him his duties. He is content to give it his whole loyalty. By contrast, in **Kingdom-religion** the believer is an artist who finds that he or she must make it all up for herself. The 1890s aesthete's idea that one's own life could become a work of art returned from about 1969 in the work of such varied figures as Gilbert and George, Richard Long, Cindy Sherman and Tracey Emin.

Autological and Heterological thinking. The human self is a relatively late creation, and even yet is not fully unified. We are not quite ourselves, even yet. People still use phrases like 'body, mind and spirit'. For nearly all of human history hitherto, people lacked the strength to think about themselves and about the human condition in a head-on, direct way. Instead, they resorted to a roundabout, objectifying. 'heterological' kind of thinking which made the topic seem to be more bearable. Thus, instead of trying to think their own deaths head-on (which is still difficult, even today), they asked for, and were indeed told, a story about how human beings long ago had forfeited their own immortality. Similarly, instead of asking why the female, which is biologically the more basic and

6

important of the two sexes, is amongst us and everywhere else in our world ancillary to and subject to the male, they typically asked for, and got, a story about how long ago women fell and lost their original equality and freedom. Such stories suggest that things came to be the way they are long ago, in the beginning, and we need to accept that things are now what they are.

Heterological, mythical-religious, thinking is still the norm today. Thus a modern professor of physics who seeks to interest the public in modern physical cosmology still feels that he must speak of the Big Bang as 'the Creation' – even though that term is wildly out of context, and indeed plain *wrong*.

The Autonomy of Religion. Autonomy is the state or condition of being a law unto oneself. One is no longer a minor, under authority and having to obey moral rules prescribed by Nature or by Tradition or by God, but instead makes and lives by rules that one has freely chosen and adopted for oneself, because they are rational. Morality doesn't *need* any external lawgiver.

During the Enlightenment – that is, roughly from Descartes to Kant, from 1630 to about 1800 – many European intellectuals rejected **Revelation** and all local Traditions as sources of knowledge. They sought instead a purely rational and universal religious outlook, a 'natural religion' rather like the 'cosmic religion' of some ancient schools of thought. They also sought a secular, non-religious theory and justification of morality.

Immanuel Kant (1724–1804) produced the most famous systematic ethical theory of the required kind, and indeed made much of the autonomy of ethics. A 1980 book of mine, originally entitled *The Autonomy of Religion*, was written as a response to the question: can we imagine a purely autonomous *religion*, or piety, independent of God and indeed independent of all ideas of religious law? English law still defines religion in terms of belief in and the worship of God, which makes life awkward for Buddhists and Jains, but surely nowadays there are many people who have a religious temperament and view of life, but do not believe in God.

Note that **autonomy** is contrasted with **heteronomy**, the state or condition of being subject to a rule of life imposed by another. See also **non-realism, Buddhism**.

B

Being, Be-ing. Ever since Old Testament times at least some religious writers have been aware of the limits of religious language, recognizing that God is strictly incomparable (Isaiah 40.25 etc.). The use of the personal pronouns cannot help but suggest that God is male, or alternatively that God is female. Believers want to think of God as hearing their prayers and responding; but an eternal being cannot *interact* with a being that lives in time.

These problems are so acute that orthodox theologians have always given priority to the *via negativa*, the 'negative way', which says the only true statements that we can make about God are denials: 'God is not-*p*'. Affirmative statements like 'God is wise' have to be very heavily qualified: the best you can say is that wisdom is predicated of a human sage in a human sort of a way, and wisdom is predicated of God in a divine sort of way. Wisdom in God differs from wisdom in a sage by the degree to which God exceeds a man – that is *infinitely*, by definition! Orthodoxy is therefore far more agnostic than most people think.

This ancient problem, sometimes called 'the crisis of representation', is now not confined to theology. It has spread everywhere. Apart from simple definitions, how does *any* descriptive language ever manage to pin down *anything* really exactly? In the years around 1911–13 at Cambridge Bertrand Russell and his young pupil Ludwig Wittgenstein were making the last great attempt to solve the problem: how can a fact-asserting sentence somehow be an exact copy of a state

8

of affairs? They were not wholly successful, and Wittgenstein eventually decided to change the question. He said, 'Don't ask what the words picture or stand for; ask instead, in the context, what *job* the utterance is being used to *do*.'

Philosophical arguments such as these, together with the modern study of living natural languages and the ways in which meanings and usages are in constant change, have had a powerful influence upon modern theology. Nobody now tries to write a straight textbook about God: the most you can do is to study human *belief* in God, and (human) uses of religious language. Nothing else is accessible to us. *Literal* or 'realistic' talk of God seems to have stopped. People don't say: 'We are praying for you'; they say: 'Our thoughts are with you at this difficult time'. In an obituary they don't write: 'God comforted him', but 'His deep religious faith comforted him at that time'. When people shift the talk from God to faith in that way, they have clearly become non-realists, even though many of them refuse to admit it.

Along these lines I publicly espoused **non-realism** in 1980, saying that we should learn to see God not as a being but as a guiding spiritual ideal, but since then I have moved on to the more general question: What is the relation between thought and being; sorry, between language and reality; sorry again, between language and its Other, non-language. Isn't non-language ineffable by definition?

What *is* non-language? It is hard to see the question, because in everyday life people's vision of the world is so plastered over with language. Imagine that you are driving down through France with your family. A child says: 'Look! Cows!' You say: 'No, we are in France. Here they are *vaches*.' The child is very cross, because she has assumed that words are stuck rigidly to what they designate, whereas you are trying to give the child the idea that the link between language and reality is purely a matter of local social convention. It is not rigid, nor is it 'natural'. And what about words such as 'nobody', which, as Alice realized, don't seem to stick to *anything*? Getting *really* awkward, let's now ask the question: What is the extra-linguistic thing out there to which we are trying to apply the words 'cows' and '*vaches*'? And to what fact out there does the sentence: 'Nobody was in the room' apply? Both questions to be answered, please, without using language!

I have always been bothered by these questions – both the theological one: 'How is talk about God, or about *any* supernatural reality possible?' and the more general, philosophical one. I have used the word 'Being' for the continuously outpouring flux of world stuff that we try to capture and describe in our various languages. When I wrote 'Be-ing', I was trying to stress that all real being, all of existence, is temporal, strung out in time. When I have written ~~Being~~, I have been trying to stress that properly speaking, if Being is non-language, there can't be a word for it, in which case 'Being' is not a proper word, and needs to be crossed out.

In the Bible (Genesis 1.1–3), before language hits it there is nothing but Chaos. The earth is 'without form and void'. God's language, in a series of commanding shouts, builds an ordered world. Today, the situation is not very different. *Our* conversation builds and continuously modifies *our* world. So the old religious myth was close to the truth of the situation, after all. Chaos, or 'prime matter', is pretty much the same as what I have called 'the dance of possibilities in the Void' or what modern physics calls 'quantum fluctuations in the vacuum'. Forget about absolute Being and absolute Nothingness; instead, blur together the dance of the possible and the minimally actual, a faint spitter and spatter of particles popping in and out of existence at absolute zero temperature. That's the starting point. See also **Analogy**.

Life is Bitterbittersweet. Since mid-Victorian times, and especially since the Second World War, much of religious language has come to be refocused around life, rather than God. This has a big influence on the traditional 'problem of evil'. God was supposed to be both unmixed perfection *and* the universal creator, so it was very hard to see why he should tolerate any evil in the world at all.

Life is very different. It is like a soap opera – endless, baggy, shapeless but extremely capacious, finite but containing all degrees of good and evil, order and disorder, beauty and ugliness, good fortune and misfortune. It is offered to us as a package deal, but the deal cannot be renegotiated, nor is there any sense in blaming life. We must love it, live it and – when the time comes – relinquish it, just as it is. Bittersweet? – no: bitterbittersweet, because we know all along that it must end. Even the happiest marriage is haunted by **death**, as the vows remind us. Death may in many cases give people a merciful release from their sufferings, but it also ends all our happiness. It is the exceptional clarity with which she sees and accepts this that makes the surviving writing of **Etty Hillesum** (q. v.) so remarkable. In a strange way, the bitter bitterness actually *heightens* the sweetness. Compare this with the traditional Christian theme of joy in affliction.

Buddhism was until surprisingly recently not well understood in the West, and not clearly distinguished from Hinduism. Only in the twentieth century did Western religious thought begin to recognize just how profoundly it challenges many entrenched Western assumptions. Buddhism, for example, really *is* non-theistic – especially in the Tibetan 'yellow-hat' (*gelugpa*) tradition to which the Dalai Lamas belong – whereas Westerners tend to assume that all religion must be theocentric, because the faiths they've known longest – Jewish, Christian and Muslim – are so. For Westerners, religion involves dependence upon divine Grace and forgiveness of our sins, whereas Buddhists typically stress self-reliance and the need to seek freedom from the inner confusion caused by a false picture of the world, and by the violence of our passions. And whereas in the Western tradition there has been a tendency for philosophical and religious thought to separate, in Asia the two have remained close, and notable books have been written about the relation to Buddhism of Heidegger, Wittgenstein, and Derrida. Many recent Western philosophers have said that the classic Buddhist view of the self is simply correct. This may be the only case of a major religious doctrine actually being true!

Still more striking is the following puzzle: Ever since Saint Paul, Christian writers have been wont to claim that Christian ethics follows 'logically' from Christian doctrine. If so, how can it be that although Buddhist doctrine is on so many fundamental points the opposite of Christian doctrine, their styles of personal holiness and of mystical prayer can be so remarkably similar? Buddhist monks and nuns I have known are not only obviously 'holy' by top Christian standards, but are evidently able to be so with a degree of wit and levity that is very rare indeed amongst Christians.

How can that be? Some Western writers still try to claim that Buddhists are theists of a veiled kind. My own approach has been rather to claim that Western talk about God and 'Middle-Way' Buddhist talk about Nothingness are in the end not so very different from each other. Both are spoken of as being beyond all images, infinite, simple and incomprehensible. Both are dark and empty, and both have the effect of unselfing the meditator, emptying one out into void bliss. Where's the difference? Only in the external packaging that every religion develops. In the early art, Jesus may be portrayed as a robed wandering philosopher, and the Buddha as a solar disc. Both may be considered as being so holy that they can be represented only by a pair of footprints or an empty chair. Both become cosmic figures.

In short, study of the relations between Christian and Buddhist language and piety is in itself an education in religious thought. The 'objective reality' of God seems to be very important in dogmatic theology, but disappears in mystical writing. See also **Mysticism etc.**

Solitary Buddhas. Christianity maintains that, in order to attain salvation, the sin-bound individual needs a Redeemer and a divine **Revelation** of saving **Truth** about what the Redeemer has done for us, and how we can lay hold of it. Somewhat similarly, Buddhists normally regard it as necessary to attach oneself to a teacher of a good lineage. But because **Buddhism** is so rationalistic, Nagarjuna (one of the two or three greatest Buddhist philosophers, c.100–300 AD) maintains that in principle the whole way to Enlightenment could be worked out and followed successfully by an independent individual of sufficient energy and persistence. In principle, the whole path to salvation is discoverable 'by reason alone':

> When Buddhas don't appear
> And their followers are gone,
> The wisdom of awakening
> Bursts forth by itself.

Etty Hillesum, a young Jewish woman of Deventer, Netherlands, who died in Auschwitz, is a remarkable Western example of such a person. She found her own way to sanctity in the last two years or so of her short life (1914–43), with little or no support or guidance of any kind from organized religion or religious professionals. There is some influence from Eckhart and from C. G. Jung, but one is astonished by the confidence with which she sets about *making it* on her own, under the pressure of a violent death which she clearly saw looming ever closer but refused to flee from.

C

Charisma is a good example of the many technical theological terms that have recently become current in ordinary language, often in a novel sense. (*Icon, iconic* is the most striking example.) A *charis* in Greek is a favour. In the New Testament *charismata* are special divinely given powers or graces or 'gifts of the Holy Spirit'. In modern use people called 'charismatic' are thought of as having compelling personal attractiveness. They are 'stars' or 'celebrities' whose 'star-power' can be used to win public support for a cause or an opinion.

The sociologist Max Weber made a useful distinction between two kinds of religious leadership. *Institutional* leaders have authority in virtue of the office to which they have been appointed. Priests of every kind and rank are the standard examples. *Charismatic* leaders – typically prophets – have authority because of their special individual gifts.

Unusually, the late Pope John Paul II was a strong – and of course 'traditional' – *institutional* leader, whilst also possessing personal *charisma* of the new secular kind. Radical theologians are in a more awkward position. They hold that standard institutional orthodoxy is simply not true. If it *were* true, the radicals would be delighted to be traditional institutional types. But it is not. In order to find true religion, the radical theologian seeks to go back into the origins of his own religious tradition, because at the point of origin of any great tradition all leadership is necessarily charismatic. John the Baptist, Jesus, and (20 years after Jesus) Paul, James and Peter were all originally charismatic. These latter figures received their own charisma and apostolic mission directly from the risen Lord: but then the phrase 'apostolic succession' shows charismatic leadership turning into institutional leadership.

Given this theoretical position, it is not surprising that most of the leading radical theologians since D. F. Strauss have been New Testament scholars. Recognizing that in the beginning a smallish group of creative individuals made it all up may inspire us to think that we can and should now re-invent all of it.

Christian Buddhism. I first used this phrase to describe my approach to Christian doctrine in 1980. It caused some offence, but my critics were mistaken.

The popular view of Christian dogmatic beliefs makes them into a crudely objectified and compulsory ideology, to which one is duty-bound to give one's assent. This highly propositional view of faith as 'belief *that*' became dominant early in the second Christian millennium. The Creeds, however, say 'I believe *in*', which puts the emphasis upon personal

14

commitment. In more recent times, and especially since the Enlightenment and the work of Kant, theologians began to argue that Christian doctrines are *regulative*, that is, their job is not so much to give us supernatural information, as rather to regulate or guide the way we live. Look at Saint Paul on the Resurrection: he knows nothing of the Empty Tomb, but instead moves on every time straight from 'Christ is risen' to: 'It's about time *you* started living a risen life'. Similarly, to believe that Christ 'will come again in glory to judge both the quick and the dead' is not to forecast a future event, but to acknowledge that one should be vigilant and live an examined life, ready for audit at any time.

On this view, religious beliefs are 'rules of life dressed up in pictures', as Wittgenstein puts it. To return to **Buddhism**, the Buddha himself insists that we should be ready to postpone or set aside the great questions of metaphysics, such as whether there is a God or not, and instead we should just get on with walking along the Way. The right Path comes first, and right doctrine comes second; or in Christian terms, *lex orandi, lex credendi*, the law of praying is the law of believing.

So there is a very strong argument *from traditional premisses* for the view that practice should come before theory, in Christianity as in Buddhism. So I tried to argue in my earliest publications during the 1960s. Overt **non-realism** was a more explicit and thoroughgoing version of the same idea, and even less popular; but I could still have defended the orthodoxy of my views as late as the 1980s. If I had wished to do so: in fact I was influenced by Ruth Robinson, widow of John Robinson, the author of *Honest to God*, who told me that John had been wrong in trying to 'row back' after his notoriety in the 1960s, as if he still hoped to be rehabilitated by the system that had ruined him. In short: *Never, ever*, retract! Not one inch.

Classical Christianity is now our Old Testament. A statement that I first published in 1980. Classical Church-type Christianity originally developed, it seems, out of the rivalry between James, Peter and Paul for leadership of the little community of Jesus' surviving followers. It provided an explanation of Jesus' death, and its purpose was to fill the interim period before Jesus' hoped-for return. Its function was disciplinary: you were to understand that Jesus had been exalted to the supernatural world (rather as Enoch and Elijah had been), and he was now the Messiah-designate. Before long he would return to establish his kingdom on earth, and it was very important that the little community should remain vigilant and orderly, accepting the leadership of James in Jerusalem, of Paul amongst the gentiles and of Peter most of all.

This earliest Christianity was then an interim arrangement, very much oriented towards the supernatural world and its own 'Advent hope'. '*Maranatha*' (Our Lord, come!), cried the waiting believers. But as time went by the Church became more institutionalized, and the coming *Kingdom* of Christ *on earth* was gradually forgotten. The Church, its priesthood and its sacraments developed into a great salvation-machine which purified souls, tanked them up with divine Grace and despatched them to join Jesus in heaven. No longer was Jesus coming to join *us* on earth: we were going to join *him* in 'heaven'. Weirdest of all, heaven was the 'Church Triumphant': no longer a temporary arrangement, the Church was now a permanent cosmic Fact. Indeed, in its own eyes the Church just *was* Christianity embodied.

What has made fully developed Church-Christianity obsolete has been, above all else, the end of the old supernaturalistic philosophy of history. The Reformation controversies encouraged the development of modern critical-historical writing, of which Thucydides in antiquity had been the greatest pioneer. But when one goes over to the modern view of history, Church-Christianity really *has* passed its sell-by date. The old image of Jesus as the Christ (the anointed one, the promised Messiah) who is to come again at the end of the world begins to look just like the image of Arthur as *rex quondam rexque futurus*, the once and future King. A touching belief, which a Victorian poet might recycle with reference to Francis Drake: but it's not where we are now.

Most of my writing since 1980 has been implicitly post-ecclesiastical. It has been a long series of experiments, trying to open up the long-awaited, half-forgotten, next dispensation. I have often called it '**Kingdom theology**' and it is of course, as it was always expected to be, secular and immediate. A corollary of this is that one should make a fresh attempt to understand the teaching of Jesus and ask how far Quakers, anarchists, communists and others have already been able successfully to appropriate a modern incarnation of his message. (They haven't: not quite.)

I love classical Christianity and did not actually cease to be a communicant until 1 October 2008, when I had become old enough (74) to realize that I *must* do so, by way of publicly giving up the notion of '**life after death**' and accepting that because we are already in the last world we must find our religious fulfilment in this life only. My remaining job is to die a **solar** death, fully accepting that this is so and that it is actually *better* this way.

Coming out. From Plato onwards (and versions of the same idea are to be found in the Hebrew Bible and in Saint Paul), much of Western thought was dominated by the appearance/reality distinction, especially in ethics and spirituality. A person's appearance is external, visible, shallow, transient, whereas the truth about him was internal, unseen and known only to himself and God, deep and lasting. You turned to God by seeking silence and solitude, shutting your eyes, folding your hands to symbolize your powerlessness and recollecting yourself. You withdrew into your own interior or spiritual life, a realm in which the only realities are your own soul and God.

To this day American prisons are called 'penitentiaries'. The idea was that solitary confinement would force the prisoner to confront himself-before-God. He would repent and turn over a new leaf. Similarly, many or most middle-class people to this day wish to conceal the most important truths about themselves: especially their income, their real feelings and their sexuality. These things are, as it is said, 'kept in the closet' and private.

A contrary view has become prominent in the last half-century. Gay people especially want to 'come out' in public. This is a profound modern imperative, and it is very prominent in my **solar ethics**. True religion is not to have a second secret identity like a spy, but to come out into the open and put on a brave show. Interestingly, both spiritualities are to be found side by side in the so-called 'Sermon on the Mount'. The original Jesus taught the solar ethics of Matthew 5.14–16. The Church later taught the spirituality of concealment set out in Matthew 6.1–21. They are diametrically opposed.

Amazingly, nobody in the past noticed that the Church had decided to follow a Way the direct opposite of Jesus' own. The Council of Trent (1545–63), indeed, actually condemned Jesus' teaching of pure, excessive love. Fjodor Dostoyevsky, in the famous chapter about the Grand Inquisitor in his *Brothers Karamazov*, comes closest to the point. The Church is actually based on a denial – or perhaps, an indefinite deferral – of Jesus' core message! Odd. See also **The Jesus of History** etc.

D

Death, Life, Eternal life, Life after death, A living death and **A dying life. 'Christian life is life after life after death'.** The polarity between life and death (with 'life after death' and 'eternal life' offering alternative syntheses of the two opposites) has always been a prominent theme of religious thought and symbolism. Naturally enough, people have seen a rhythmic oscillation between life and death both in the annual cycle of the seasons and in the succession of human generations. Even sober Western philosophers, from Plato to Bishop

Joseph Butler in the eighteenth century, have been so weak-headed as to suggest that the renewal of life each Spring and the emergence from its chrysalis of the adult butterfly offer us some kind of reason for believing that we too may be able to re-emerge from death.

In fact, in the whole of Western philosophy there has only ever been one moderately sensible argument for life after death, namely the suggestion that if our rationality is a participation in an eternal rational order or Logos that pervades the whole Cosmos, then it may be possible for us to pass away beyond ourselves into a transpersonal immortality of Reason. Some such idea as this has been taken seriously by many good philosophers, including such major figures as Aristotle, Spinoza and Hegel. Rapt in the enjoyment of great art – especially music – I have always inclined to the solution described since 1985 as **solar living**. Forget introversion, the cult of subjectivity and the attempt to save one's soul. Instead, live a dying life, that is, live generously, live expressively, live by self-outing, like a fire or like the sun. If one can learn to live with sufficient heedless, carefree generosity, one will simply not worry about death, for one is living 'a dying life'. The original source of this idea must be Saint Paul, who despite his poor modern reputation can occasionally rise to great heights (2 Corinthians 6.1–10; 1 Corinthians 4.8–13). Traditionally, the believer underwent a symbolic death and rebirth at baptism: thus, the entire Christian life was *already* post mortem. One keeps always the knowledge of universal transience, but death as such has lost its sting. Love, religious or secular, does not literally *conquer* or abolish death, but it can free us from the *fear* of death.

The Death of God. An idea that has been popular for about 200 years. Around the time of the French Revolution and the philosophies of Kant and Schopenhauer, Western philosophy seems to have broken away permanently from God. This is partly because, after the Enlightenment, the new sense of history, the Industrial Revolution and radical politics seemed to picture Man as being not the inhabitant of a fixed divine framework for his life, but rather as the maker of his own knowledge, his own history and his own social order. Secondly, there were very few events remaining in which people promptly read the hand of God. On the contrary, the 'horizontal' or naturalistic kind of explanation typical of natural science had come to seem much more powerful and interesting. As soon as the huge potential of powered industrial machinery and transport was grasped, people began to see human technology as a maker of history. At the same time, the old world-view which thought in terms of relatively unchanging substances and 'the fixity of species' began to be replaced by ideas of temporal process and 'development' or 'evolution'. Everything begins to be seen as a product of history – perhaps especially language, ideas and even human emotions and styles of piety. All unchanging 'absolutes', including all absolute presuppositions or assumptions, find themselves being questioned and 'relativized'.

Against this background it is scarcely surprising that God was in question throughout the nineteenth century and especially after *philosophical* criticism of God (for being an eternal, unchanging Substance, who couldn't easily be thought of as caring about us) joined hands with biblical criticism, radical politics and biological evolution.

F. W. Nietzsche (1846–1900) did *not* announce that the **Death** of God had just occurred. It was for him one of the greatest events in human history, and it would take two centuries to arrive and be understood fully. It had already happened, around 1790. Nietzsche, about 1885, was trying to awaken people to it, and the full impact of the Death of God would be felt by the late twentieth century.

It has all turned out pretty much as Nietzsche predicted. During the 1960s the Death-of-God theology appeared, and Nietzsche himself replaced Marx as the single most important modern prophet. All **Grand Narratives** about the march of all things towards a Better World to Come began to die. Moral **realism** broke down. **Postmodernism** arrived,

20

and the two-centuries-old 'decline of religion' accelerated sharply. Painting went black and was replaced at its leading edge by conceptual art, which has not budged since.

This sudden upheaval of the 1960s to the 1990s has influenced not only 'Western' and Christian or Jewish societies, but also other faiths. With dismay, the older generation see the young rejecting the traditional patriarchal social and sexual order and becoming anarchic. In response there has been a sharp neo-conservative reaction in many faiths – perhaps, in *all* faiths – which utters dire threats and battles to reimpose traditional values and structures. It is often called 'fundamentalism'. It is repressive and full of hate.

I have sought a mediating role, which welcomes our postmodern emancipation from the traditional patriarchal order and recognizes that the intellectual breakdown of the old religious orthodoxy has occurred and is final. The old metaphysical God of the philosophers, the old Absolute Author/Authority, is indeed gone and cannot be reinstated. But we can perhaps describe a new kind of religion for our age which really does work. We may see God as a guiding spiritual ideal, of the sort that I call 'a *leading* idea': a goal of mystical aspiration, the traditional 'pearl of great price'. We may accept that the 'Church' period of Western history, a period of social discipline, is now over and it's time to move on to the post-ecclesiastical period to which the Society of Friends, the Quakers, have long borne witness. For them God is no longer 'above' us, but has become 'democratized' and is immanent within everyone's reason and conscience. Sometimes I confess that I still love the dead God, just as I still love my dead parents. Most recently, I have begun trying to break away from the remnants of the idea of God as an infinite substance. Instead I see God as 'God everliving and everdying', a burning process, the outpouring and the utter transience of everything, into which we plunge and with which we pass joyfully away. As a new religious symbol I like, not only the Sun and the Fountain, but also the dancers of Henri Matisse. See also **Everything is a Period Piece.**

Democratic Philosophy. Especially in the period dominated by the Romantic Movement, Europeans have taken a pride in their Great Men, or 'geniuses', who have been seen as the chief setters of standards and agents of historical change. In classical antiquity there was already a certain cult of such figures, and they became the subjects of monumental statues in public places and of the first biographies, such as Plutarch's *Lives*. In antiquity the main emphasis was upon political and military greatness, but in modern Europe Giorgio Vasari in 1570 shifted the emphasis to the definition of a national canon of 'great' architects, painters and sculptors.

In nineteenth-century Europe there was a great demand in each of the emergent unified nations for a national canon of great founding artists, writers, composers and thinkers, who by embodying the national 'spirit – a 'genius' was originally a spirit that indwelt a particular place or person, so that a specially talented individual might be described as 'ingenious' – the line of such artists gave to each nation a secular version of the line of Israel's prophets in the Bible. It is very notable that in the great new historical dictionaries of the national languages, entries included a number of illustrative quotations from canonical writers. In the *Oxford English Dictionary*, for example, Shakespeare is the greatest single national 'genius', and his surviving corpus is full of thousands of examples of how the English language was used by its greatest master.

Unlike today's celebrities, who are very often female, the true European genius was almost invariably male, which perhaps helps to explain American students' resistance to the domination of their syllabuses by DWEMs, dead white European males. In Europe, at the very period when the notion of the national Genius was at its height, others began to object that the real motor of historical change was the accumulated weight of the struggles and sufferings of ordinary people or was the operation of vast impersonal forces or was a shift in the overall cultural consensus, the climate of opinion or *Zeitgeist*. Gradually, with the rise of the mass media and mass higher education and with the general democratization of culture, the notion of the 'genius' has itself been so dumbed down as to have disappeared. If hundreds of sportspeople are 'geniuses', then nobody is, and the idea is dead.

In philosophy, notice that in the whole period dominated by Platonism the philosopher was an exceptionally gifted Seer of Reason who contemplated a higher world, an order of *a priori* reason invisible to ordinary people. But the later Wittgenstein became an ordinary-language, democratized philosopher. Interestingly, Church history too has recently turned sharply away from its traditional preoccupation with top clerics, theologians, mystics, heretics and the like, and the most fashionable recent books have looked at religious change in the parishes and amongst ordinary people.

In my own writings – and especially in the three little *Everyday Speech* books of 1999/2000 – I attempted to apply the same method to religious thought, arguing that the introduction of new phrases in ordinary language, such as the remarkable new idioms in which we now talk about 'life', gives us a mappable and objective way of studying religious change. In a theoretical essay so far published only in Chinese (2008), I claimed that we have here *A New Method of Religious Studies* which, in an age when vast amounts of historical text have become readily available in machine-readable form, promises to give us at last the long-sought science of religious thought.

Again influenced by Wittgenstein's ordinary-language philosophy, I have tried to produce a democratic philosophy of my own – with what success is very doubtful. What is certainly true is that in the most recent English dictionaries the illustrations of word-use tend to be drawn, *not* from canonical Great Writers, but from the idioms of **everyday speech**. The writers describe these idioms as clichés, but they are more important and instructive than we realize. Which is a good example of the excellent rule that **language is much cleverer than the people who speak it**. In postmodern-talk, **'language speaks us'**.

Democratization in religion. Even Plato, no democrat, noticed that over a very long period, dignities and privileges which at first belonged only to the very greatest gods and kings tend to become 'democratized': they trickle down to the lower ranks in society. A good, vivid example is the hope of attaining happiness and security in the Underworld after death in ancient Egypt. At first, it was the Pharaoh who in death was united with the god Osiris, but gradually this blessing came to be enjoyed by lesser mortals too, until eventually everybody was joined in death to the god of the Underworld. Another example: who makes the law that binds you? Originally, the god. Later the king and then the Senate or Congress. But eventually, you yourself at last achieve moral autonomy. Hegel sums up the whole mighty historical process: 'Once, one was free; then, some were free; finally, all will be free.'

How does this process of democratization happen? In most cultures it seems that there is a social heaven of sacred or royal persons, or stars or celebrities. They seem to function as 'role-models': we copy these people and dream of becoming like them. Our dreams guide our hopes and our strivings, until in the end they become self-fulfilling.

It is in this sense that I call religious ideas *leading* ideas. Ask yourself who in the Bible has a flying-machine with which he can jet around in the sky? God in Ezekiel 1, Elijah in 2 Kings 1.9–12 . . . Now you get it: today *we all of us* have access to aerial chariots. That's democratization.

In religion, revolutionaries and radical reformers are always people who want to push history along faster and to accelerate the process of democratization. Following Wyclif and Huss, they criticize the exactions and the arrogance of the hierarchy (a word that literally means, *rule by high priests*). To see what they want, look at the beautiful democracy of an old English Quaker graveyard.

How does one achieve full religious democracy? As the Old Testament prophets say, by fully internalizing God within each human being, so that God is no longer an Other, over against us. God and the self are fully concentric, so that God is the same thing as the larger Self that in your later life you should be slowly growing into. His clarity on this last point is the best bit of the religious thought of Carl Jung. Nearly all radical theologians will accept the general argument of this entry. They all want religious democratization. See also **Mysticism etc.**

E

Earthshine, backlighting. A word I use to make the point that, contrary to what some people say, we do *not* have any privileged access to and knowledge of a private inner space inside our own heads. The moon is not itself luminous at all: the light with which it appears to shine is the sun's light bouncing back off it. In addition, when only a crescent moon is visible, the remainder of the lunar disc is often visible, backlit with Earthshine – that is light that has bounced from the Sun to the Earth and then from the Earth to the Moon and then back to us on Earth.

Similarly, I maintain that your primary field of lit-up consciousness is simply your field of view. Hence, **Your mind is in front of your face**. In the field of view intellectual 'seeing' and optical seeing are always interwoven, as our language shows in great detail. From this glowing and vividly conscious realm a certain backlight is shed back into our subjectivity. It faintly illumines an 'interior' world that we can discern or make out only with the help of 'external' lighting and imagery. Thus the inner world has no light of its own. We know it only backlit. Our picture of our own interiority is a (very variable) metaphorical construct – *from outside.*

In working out my views, I am rejecting the traditional vocabulary of **introversion**, which has us withdrawing into our own interior space in order to find our true selves and God, and instead I am making the direction of movement *always* outgoing or **extravertive**. This has a big effect upon my whole vocabulary, and I start using words like **expressivism, expressionism** and **emotivism** (the word 'emotion', literally *movement out*, was once used to mean emigration!) The picture is always of language pouring out of us and differentiating the constructed human world. '**Can you tell what it is** that you are looking at?' means at once: 'Can you **make out?**' and 'Can you *describe* what it is?' Our seeing of the world is always also our construal and construction of the world: we see in sentences, and here I quote the extraordinary speed with which a sports commentator can describe the action before him. He seems already to have it in sentences even as it is occurring.

In conclusion, I have turned sharply away from my own early emphasis on subjectivity or self-consciousness, inspired by Kierkegaard and the mystics of the inner life. I now see the whole life of the soul as outgoing, expressive and communicative. Forget your inner life! It was a fantasy. Get up off your knees, open your eyes and get out more! There was *no* real you inside your head. **We live along the wires** and are ourselves in our communicative relations with other people. Another way of making the same point is to say that if you know me, your interpretation of me is probably just as good as my own interpretation of myself. I don't really have any important evidence that is not equally available to you. I have no privileged access to my own internal space.

The general philosophical point to remember is that on the account I have given, thought and being, or more exactly language and reality, are *always already* interwoven.

Easy, going. A phrase often misread. I do *not* mean merely easy-going. I mean untroubled about one's own transience. For most of their history, humans were transient nomads, anyway. Then we settled into fixed territories, with cities and stone Temples, and we began to believe in stability and 'roots'. In time we began to seek absolute permanence and to suspect and devalue everything vagrant and fleeting. One of the most striking of the apocryphal sayings of Jesus is: '**Be**

passers-by' (Gospel of Thomas 42). Travel lightly. Aren't cut flowers, which are already dying, nevertheless overwhelmingly more beautiful than plastic ones? So be happy to be just a transient mortal: it's better than the alternative.

Ecstatic immanence. 'Ecstasy' is standing or jumping outside or beyond one's normal limits. 'Immanence' is the state of being completely immersed or embedded within one's world, without pretending to be able to jump clear of it in any way. In 'a philosophy of immanence' everything is explained 'naturally' or internally, without any felt need to seek any external grounding or attachment.

The phrase 'ecstatic immanence' is thus at first sight paradoxical. It refers to the great happiness one may feel when one gives up various kinds of aspiration after transcendent 'absolutes' or 'foundations' and instead returns into ordinariness. The jump back into ordinariness – for which I have coined the word **entostasy** – can seem like a joyful return to sanity and freedom, as when, for example, a former priest finds that an ordinary woman is a more tangible and wholesome love object than the Blessed Virgin he used to pray to.

Emotivism. Usually, the ethical theory that regards our moral and evaluative judgements as expressions of feeling rather than as reporting supposed facts about objective moral or aesthetic values. This is not quite exact, for our language shows that we can and do *'feel that* p' – that is, our feelings are often at least implicitly propositional. When I describe something as 'charming' or 'frightening' or as 'completely unacceptable', I seem to claim that there are facts about it that explain *why* it has such-and-such an effect on me and would have the same effect on many or most other people. I have good grounds for feeling as I do.

That point aside for the moment, I regard the life of the self in time as powered by a constant outflow of varied and mixed feelings, feelings that may be 'turned on by' or 'enhanced by' or for that matter 'nauseated by' the various things we encounter. Now all the words and phrases in the language have various feeling responses annexed to them, so that our own feeling responses guide us and help us to find the words that fit on every occasion. Thus our feelings help to colour up the world and are vital in shaping our descriptions of things. To that extent we are all of us **artists**, in the sense that our basic response to life and our world building is highly self-involving and emotive and quite unlike the cool detachment of scientific description.

This **emotive–expressive** view of the life of the self in time is, as I say, typical of the dynamic-depth psychology of Freud and Jung and also of art. But I don't in the least agree with the anti-scientism of some modern philosophers, because of course for certain purposes the cool, analytical scientific gaze is very productive and powerful. That is undoubtedly true. But you'd be a sad creature if you kept your own feelings out of it *all* the time.

Emptiness. In Buddhist philosophy, usually the view that there is no substantial, enduring, independent being of things. There are no *substances*, in the Western sense. The true vision of the world sees only 'the veil of sense', an endless stream or web of shimmering sense-experiences, as in a late Claude Monet painting. In Anglo-Saxon philosophy a similar view is called 'phenomenalism'.

In Buddhist philosophy the human self is usually Empty: that is, it is not a simple, naturally immortal, spiritual substance, a rational soul, but just a collection or 'aggregate' of different capacities or abilities. I have agreed with that view since the early 1980s, and therefore have long abandoned ideas of **life after death**. Since Monet's late paintings give me such pleasure, I see no reason why we shouldn't regard the vision of the world, as nothing more than a stream of empty phenomena, as being blissful. To take the same idea further, colour-field abstract painting, or just gazing into the blue sky, can have a powerful effect of blissfully emptying out and drowning the self. Hence my phrases commending **the discipline of the Void** and **making a friend of the Void**. Good way to make friends with **death**, too.

Recently, I have tried to apply these ideas about Emptiness to God, saying that when we give up the philosophy of substance we may learn to see God as an endless outpouring: 'everliving, everdying'. In which case, **the Death of God** is not an event in the *human* history of ideas, but the way God always lives, by pouring silently out and passing away all the time. True, that makes God temporal: but if all being is temporal, then God has to be temporal too.

Energetic Spinozism. A name I have used since about 1995 to describe my philosophy. Baruch Spinoza (1632–77) of Amsterdam was a generation or so younger than Descartes. Whereas the British saw the chief characteristic of the new physics as being its appeal to experience/experiment, Descartes and Spinoza were more impressed by its mechanistic and rigorously mathematical character. They both developed rationalistic systems of thought. Descartes tried to avoid conflict with the Church and stayed close to the traditional accounts of God and the human soul as laid down by Augustine. Spinoza moved away from all ideas of a natural/supernatural distinction and a special divine **revelation** in history to just one people and was accordingly ejected from the Synagogue. Spinoza describes all of reality as a single eternal divine substance, 'God or Nature', which has many attributes and expresses itself in many different modes. God's intellect is impersonal and all its workings are necessary. In the loving contemplation of and union with the divine intellect lies our highest – indeed our eternal – happiness. It is an intellectual rapture.

Later generations used the name 'Spinozism' to mean, roughly, post-orthodox cosmic religiosity, or perhaps a scientist's feeling for the Sublime in modern cosmology. My version of Spinozism is also naturalistic, but in a more biological vocabulary. I don't talk of eternity, substance and self-unfolding Reason, but about an everlasting Fountain of outpouring energies and feelings that come out into **expression** – especially, as language – and pass away. My vision is not purely intellectual, but flowing, temporalized and emotive, perhaps because when young I studied biology for five years. See also **The Fountain**.

Eschatological urgency. Early Christianity had a sense of urgency. 'How long, O Lord?': in short, 'Hurry up, God!' The End, it was hoped, would come soon. The apostle says, '*While we have time*, let us do good unto all men . . .' (Galatians 6.12).

In modern times belief in **life after death** has rather abruptly and completely ended and that urgency has returned in a new form. As Heidegger remarked, death, making life finite, calls upon us to hurry up and get on with our life's chief task. In the year in which I write, I shall be 77. I'm in a great hurry, not least because, like many people nowadays, I made rather a late start. In recent years I have been conscious of needing a little more time to finish my work. Notice here that all ideas of a love of one's life and of a life's work presuppose that we understand and accept that life is finite. We have just about enough time for one great thing in our lives.

At the other end of the scale are those impatient people who try to speed God up, to accelerate the historical process. They want the End, the glorious climax, the Revolution, their own union with God, to come, and *fast*. They include a wide range of mystics, revolutionaries and terrorists. The similarity of aim between mystics and terrorists was first pointed out by the French philosopher Jean Baudrillard.

Everyday Speech. For many years I have noticed that sophisticated philosophical points are often made in a very compressed way in the familiar phrases of everyday speech. For example, we have recently come to use the word 'perception' in a novel way, to mean 'interpretation', as when we talk about 'the Chinese perception of human rights issues'. Another example is the use of **'make out'** to mean 'discern' or 'descry' when we are straining our eyes as we try to 'make out' what something is. These are examples of a bit of modern philosophy – we don't just passively record or register our experience; we actively interpret it in order to make it **make sense** and so build our worlds – that has somehow managed to get into ordinary language. How? I think that we adopt and help to establish a new idiom if we find that it is often *le mot juste*, it's helpful to us. Thus a kind of Darwinian natural selection tests new idioms and works in favour of good ones, helping them to *catch on* and so become entrenched in our speech. Furthermore, the sheer abundance of our modern communications enables new idioms to spread around the world with astonishing speed.

Noticing this I wrote the three short *Everyday Speech* books of 1999–2000 and in the following years a number of others along similar lines, suggesting that we have here the beginnings of a new method of studying the movement of *Geist*, the world of ideas, and even perhaps one day a new theology.

A curious synchrony: in *Cosmopolis*, the US novelist Don de Lillo has a page saying just what I say about the word **It**, quite independently. And a PPS: synchrony is a Jungian term for very striking coincidences in the world of thought. An everyday example is the case where somebody telephones me just as I am thinking about him. Nietzsche uses the term 'star friendship' for the case where the development of their thinking brings two people very close together for a while. Subsequently they drift apart, but a bond of star friendship remains between them.

Evil. The cosmological-dualist philosophy of history, originating in ancient Persia, spread to Judaism, to Christianity and thence into the Romantic historicism that swept the West after Hegel. All history is seen as a long struggle between the opposed powers of light and darkness, but after the coming Last Battle the evil empire will be chained up for ever, and the good people (our lot, in case you were wondering) will enjoy perpetual peace and happiness in a purified and perfected world.

The whole way of thinking involved here seems to come naturally to ordinary people, especially in theistic cultures, and it is still popular. There must be a Power for Good, surely, and if so is it not reasonable that there should also be a Power of Evil; and if God is almighty and good, he must in the end overcome Evil finally, surely? Many people still argue along such lines. However, I have argued that formerly vivid God idioms in our language have now been almost entirely replaced by life idioms, and especially since the 1960s as old-style belief in God has gone into accelerating decline. Instead of asking after a disaster 'Why did God let it happen?' we now prefer to say, **'Life's a package deal** that we cannot renegotiate. Death and mischance are part of the package and **that's it.'**

As a result, we have suddenly stopped complaining to God about evil – or at least, we do much less of it. The old dream of a total and permanent victory over evil is now dead. We can do something to diminish evil by applied science, good politics and progressive social reform and so we should. In my own philosophy I argue that our chief religious problem now is not what to do about sin and suffering ('moral' and 'physical' evil), but the bigger and more general issue of what is called **'metaphysical evil'**: finitude, time and death. I answer that **'solar living'** is the right way to **say Yes to life** and to be happy all the way into death. It is the best answer, but there remains a touch of **bitterbittersweetness** about it. But this touch of anguish can actually *heighten* our joy in life.

Expression. Literally, squeezing out – as for example when a young mother 'expresses' milk from her breast and puts it in a bottle, to feed the baby with later. Paintings are often thought of as, and often intended to be, expressions of the feelings or the subjectivity of the painter. Hence **expressionism** in art. I have tried to persuade people to see religious activity in an expressionist way. By acting out or expressing our feelings with the help of religious rituals and symbols, we can help to synthesize or resolve our conflicting feelings and so get ourselves together. Jung in particular describes an artist's works, viewed in chronological succession, as a developing series of self-expressions that together make up an objectified spiritual autobiography. Consider the example of Rembrandt's self-portraits. Similarly, a French-style *journal intime* may be written as an attempt at, and a record of, self-forging.

Introvertive and Extravertive religion and mysticism. Introvertive piety 'turns inward', away from the senses, away from human company and away from all merely human images of the divine. One withdraws into inner emptiness and silence, listening out for God in the dark. This was the classic *via negativa*, the Way of Negation, standard in Christian mysticism until the beginnings of a turn to this life and to the emotions that began in the towns in the later Middle Ages. It is a kind of spirituality that converges with **Buddhism**, and indeed I myself have repeatedly insisted that at top level God = Nothingness, because the two cannot be distinguished by us. (Remember, orthodoxy insists that God is incomprehensible because he transcends the categories of our thinking.)

Extravertive piety 'turns outward' (unfortunately most people now write 'extrovert') to see the world 'charged with the grandeur of God' (G. M. Hopkins). This Affirmative Way, the *via affirmativa*, is particularly strong in the English love of landscape and 'nature', and one may quote familiar examples from Traherne, Blake, Palmer and many Victorian poets – but above all, Hopkins. The most popularly accessible example of all is of course Vincent van Gogh, in whose strongly religious vision the most everyday objects and sights throb with a burning intensity.

I have described many personal experiences of this kind and in connection with it have coined several expressions; in particular **the mysticism of secondariness** and **glory**. Perhaps the modern popular use of the Greek word **charisma** (grace) belongs in this context, too.

With the end of Platonism, the old introvertive mysticism has become, at least for me, **the discipline of the Void**. One knows now that there is nothing there, so one deliberately

33

goes *as an exercise* into absolute nothingness. The old extravertive mysticism tends nowadays to become a rapturous high-spirited **solar joy** in **life**. For you, too?

F

Fact and Interpretation. A good friend of mine is a left-of-centre investigative journalist whose entire ethic is based on the idea of a discoverable and statable objective truth of the matter in question: 'Comment is free, but facts are sacred.' He sharply objects to my views, but I'll show why he is wrong.

To start with, a *datum* (the singular of *data*: if you ever dare to use *data* and *media* as singulars, I'll come back and haunt you), a *datum*, I repeat, is literally a thing *given*. It's from the same verb as donation. Whereas a fact is literally a thing *made*. It's from the same verb as factory. So a datum is a raw given, an uninterpreted sense-experience at the first instant of its appearance, before the mind has 'made anything' of it. Thus *listening*, plus a decision by me about what it is I'm listening *to*, equals *hearing* something; and *looking* plus a decision by me about what it is I'm looking *at*, equals *seeing* something. I take these two examples from Wittgenstein's remarks about the difference between looking and seeing and between listening and hearing, because I learnt Wittgenstein in the early 1950s, when I was just a little younger than I am now. But Kant has already got it right in 1781: to have knowledge of something in the world of experience, I have to apply concepts to intuitions. The 'intuition' is the raw tingle in a sense organ, and the concept is a general idea or word applied to it in order to *make something* of it. So we 'create facts'.

In more recent times the same point is made more forcefully. 'There are no facts, only interpretations,' says Nietzsche. 'Interpretation goes all the way down,' says Richard Rorty. I tend to put it in terms of **Be-ing** – the gentle silent outpouring of the possible, trying to get out into actuality – and the dance of language. Being fills language like a puff of wind, catching and filling out words, lifting them up and away like dandelion seeds. I talk like this because I like the modern physicists' talk of 'quantum fluctuations' in empty space. It makes all talk of absolute Being and absolute Nothingness redundant, replacing it with **featherlite** mathematics and a kind of wobble back and forth between the possible and the minimally actual. That's good: those people are seriously *bright*. Anyway, the upshot is that, in a favourite saying of mine: **'We are in the Void and we make the lot.'** That's radical **humanism**. The Real? – an everlasting dance of conflicting interpretations. **Truth?** – the mobile consensus of the best arguers about the topic under discussion.

My unfortunate friend won't have liked any of this. I'll allow that although there are no completely interpretation-free and objective facts, it is obviously true that some interpretations are to be preferred to others. Of course there *can* be rational debate about good and bad reporting and obviously the stark British Fact/Interpretation distinction is a good starting point for opening up a debate about journalistic ethics. But as the debate goes on, any confidence that the facts of the matter can be agreed by all and stated in a neutral vocabulary will soon evaporate. Try visiting Israel/Palestine.

Featherlite. A word I used in my very postmodern late 1980s, to describe the world-view that I was then learning. Sometimes I used 'ultralite'. But the word 'light' in English is remarkably ambiguous. As well as the enormous vocabulary of optical light, *lux*, and the even greater vocabulary for the metaphorical light of understanding, vision, clarity, insight and the illumination of the mind, there are also two more large vocabularies for light as *levis*, lightweight as opposed to heavy, grave, solemn or ponderous. A high spirited girl, making light of things, may be called bubbly, floaty, ditsy, dizzy. See the entry below for **Landscape Art, Eastern and Western** and recall the Japanese expression 'the floating world'.

As during the 1980s I was frightening myself by becoming steadily more nihilistic in philosophy, I cheered myself by remembering levity. Extreme lightness can be very beautiful and even exhilarating. Buddhists are very good at it. See also *Emptiness and Brightness*, 2001.

Feminism and bipolar thinking. A surprising number of words have antonyms, so many that it seems we do much of our thinking in terms of polar opposites like right and left, up and down, day and night, hot and cold and so on. What is even more striking is that the way in which we construct these oppositions is very often modelled on the way society has taught us to see the male/female distinction. In short, sexual difference, which we become aware of from a very early age, becomes the model for the way we differentiate our whole world.

How does this work? At first the world is chaotic, confused and turbid and with only patches that are relatively illuminated. To build a world, we must separate light from darkness. Let there be light! We foreground what is clear, bright, direct and stable, and we push back everything that is dark, devious and unreliable, drawing a firm line between the two regions we have created, namely light and darkness. To make this great – and perhaps primary – distinction we have used the classic male/female contrast. The male principle is 'obviously' prior, clear, direct, straight and commanding. As the phrase goes, it is *as clear as day*. The female principle, on the other hand, has to be repressed, secondary, dark and indirect. Subversive.

So it is that the victory of God over the female chaos monster (who is called *Tehom/Tiamat*, 'the Deep', in the Bible, *Grendel* by us Anglo-Saxons and 'Nessie' by the tabloid newspapers) – is also the victory of light over darkness, of man over woman. It seems that patriarchy and the subjection of woman are principles that were fundamental to the first formation of human language and culture and to our first construction of the human world. We just *are* sexist, and so is reason itself. So is religion, and so is the whole of culture.

Inevitably, heterological thinking tries to escape this by dreaming of an original matriarchy, somewhere, at some time in the past. But such myths telling of how things once were, or might have been, the other way round change nothing. They only make the masculine status quo seem the more overwhelmingly dominant and inescapable. Androcentrism (as I sometimes prefer to call it) is so profoundly built into their theology and their institutions that the three great 'Abrahamic' faiths have as yet been able to make only token efforts to free themselves from it.

If you doubt me, take a ride on one of those buses in Jerusalem in which women, *Jewish* women, are made to sit in the back. Or try to find in the whole of Christian art any serious representation *at all* of the female genitalia and of the act of giving birth: and then, when you have found that the answers are nil and nil, see how ubiquitous are representations of the male genitalia – especially those of the godman, Jesus Christ. The extent to which the whole tradition has been based upon the subjection of woman and *especially* of woman as *zoopoietes*, life giver, is astonishing. (Zoopoietes is a title of the 'masculine' Holy Spirit.)

One of the main motives for any radical theology today has to be an attempt to change these ancient ways of thinking – which means that we need to reinvent everything, starting with God, 'the Lord and giver of life'.

Fictionalism. A fiction was something feigned (*fingo*, *fictum*), a mere pack of lies, until around two to three hundred years ago, when fiction became much the most popular literary form, under such names as the novel and romance (new and untruthful, once again). For many generations, letting your daughter read novels was considered to be as dangerous as letting her go on the stage – and for much the same reason.

Against this background, it is not surprising that the gradual advance since about 1800 of a mythical interpretation first of the Old Testament, then of the Gospels and finally of Christian doctrine as a whole, should have met with such fierce resistance. A myth is a story and to say about some biblical narrative that it is mythical was to say that it is untrue and a deception.

Today, however, many theologians, including even some prominent neo-conservatives, are unapologetic fictionalists. It's a story, but it is *the* story, the best and biggest story, so we propose to make it come true by telling it out and acting it out, loud and clear. I once published an experimental fictionalist work myself, *What is a Story?* (1991), which particularly emphasized the value of stories (as also of music) in shaping life and pacing action. It had some success, unusually for me.

The Fire. We know too little about the earliest of the Greek philosophers. The one of whom I would most like to know much more is Heraclitus of Ephesus (c.535–475 BC). Here is a summary constructed from the few fragments of him that survive in quotation:

> There is no permanent reality except the reality of change. Permanence is an illusion of the senses. All things carry with them their opposites, so that death lurks everywhere in life and non-being within being, and the only real states of things are always transitional – states of becoming. Fire is the underlying substance of the Universe, and all the other elements are transformations of it. Even life, reason and the individual human soul are but modes of the universal fire.

The Fountain. In a post-metaphysical age we cannot access any deep **truth** of things, and the cosmos does not have any deep Foundation. But what I call 'poetical' philosophy and religious thought are still possible. They work by finding and elaborating powerful images which can pull together, reconcile and unify large swathes of our experience. This helps us

to make sense of the world and the human condition, rec-
onciling us to our life and helping us to see how we should
live.

I think that at the beginning and the end of the Western
tradition both Heraclitus and Nietzsche were doing a sort of
poetical philosophy. In my writing, I have made most of the
Sun, **the Fire**, the Fountain and **Life**. All of them live by dying –
they pour out and pass away and endlessly renew themselves.
God doesn't work as well as he did, and my ordinary language studies suggest that God-talk is now dying. But the
ones I have quoted make good replacements for God. See,
amongst my books, *Emptiness and Brightness*, *Solar Ethics*,
Life, Life and *The Fountain*.

Interestingly, Jesus uses much the same imagery. In all the
1330 or so sayings attributed to him, only one mentions music. Contrary to what's usually said about Judaism, the Word
and music and about the Jews as being people of the ear,
Jesus was it seems *not* a person of the ear. But he was intensely visual, and the sayings are full of sunlight, lamplight,
firelight, lightning flashes, natural beauties and so on.

The Fray. During the past decade or so I have often used the
word 'fray' when describing the way we should relish the cut
and thrust of life. We should not be afraid to mingle or to get
stuck in. We should actively enjoy mixing it – and all these
sexual metaphors, which I use very consciously, indicate that
we get and should get an almost sexual pleasure from grap-
pling with the tasks of the day.

I invoke this vocabulary deliberately, to stress that I aim to
reverse the traditional Western spirituality of preserving one's
personal integrity or wholeness by wearing white, withdrawing from social life and especially by avoiding all conflict and
all mingling of body fluids. No: we don't want the sort of soul
that shrinks from life. Our life is precisely our going-out to
others and expending ourselves.

39

G

Ghostly titles. Inside many of my books the outlines of a second and slightly different book can be made out, the book that you would be reading if the whole volume had kept its original 'ghostly title'. The first notable case of this was *Taking Leave of God* (1980), which I originally wrote to the title *The Autonomy of Religion*. My intention, dating from 1977, had been to try to do for religion what Kant had done for ethics, that is, to argue that if the moral way can and indeed should be followed freely, autonomously and just for its own sake, why shouldn't the same be said of the religious path? Faith doesn't *have* to be a conviction that something exists: it might instead – with advantage – be seen as an open, trusting attitude towards the future, or towards 'life' in general. Indeed, there are theologians who do interpret belief in God along just those lines.

As it turned out, the book was retitled by John Bowden, its publisher, who sold it very successfully as a sort of successor to John Robinson's *Honest to God* (1963), and it is still in print. But the title change meant a big change in the way the book was, and is, read. It was a shrewd change from the religious publishers' point of view, but it meant that the book's ghostly thesis has remained undiscussed.

In other cases, the new title had definite advantages. *Solar Ethics* (1995) has had some impact and the title may stick. Its ghostly title *Good Show* was intended to mark my adoption of a theatrical expressivist notion of the self and my replacement of the traditional spirituality of introversion with a new extravertive account of selfhood. We are not readymade real selves: we forge ourselves by the way we choose to present ourselves. You are your own self-presentation: get out and put on a **good show**! See also **Realism, etc.** and **Emotivism**.

Globalization. Several religions claim that their message is universal, or 'catholic' or 'ecumenical', and three great faith traditions remain missionary and multicultural: Islam, **Buddhism** and Christianity are all spreading around in our recently globalized world, with its very large-scale population shifts. (Some other faiths, such as Judaism and Sikhism, are also very widely dispersed, but nowadays they do not actively evangelize in the way they sometimes did in the past.)

This wide diffusion of the faiths in the late-modern world has some awkward consequences. When it exports ancient sectarian divisions and national traditions to new territories, it may make them appear irrational and violent. Why are people fighting so hard to maintain sectarian divisions and conflicts that do them only harm? As I write, Taliban-type Muslims have been sending suicide bombers against Sufi Muslims: where's the sense in that?

Behind all such issues is the wider issue of globalization versus localism. All of the three ancient faiths that claim to be universal are in practice found to be rooted in, and to privilege, one culture area, one ethnic group, one language and one local tradition. But full-scale globalization of the newest kind threatens in due course to assimilate and swallow up all our received differences of national, religious and ethnic tradition. Every great religion everywhere will soon be no more than a tourist attraction, a set of local folkways, stuff that (frankly) nobody any longer dreams of taking seriously.

Personally, I go along with all this and think that in reality and on the ground it has already happened. That's why my 'radical theology' goes much further than any previous one. I am now keen to be rid of every kind of identity-politics and every kind of nostalgia for tradition.

Glory. An interesting word. In its oldest Hebrew use, it meant something not far from glamour and prestige: the glow of **charisma** and international gloss that emanates from any great and rich person, or king, or god. Later, it was the brilliant light of God's own holiness that dazzles anyone who sees the divine Face. My use of the word is secularized: it means 'brightness' – the almost fluorescent shining beauty of the *consciously seen* world of our visual experience. Almost the first people to see this the way *I* see it were the great Paris school painters of the late nineteenth century. See it especially in the best *pointilliste* paintings of seaside scenes, in much of the later Claude Monet, everywhere in the mature style of van Gogh and in Matisse's great interiors. If you don't instantly recognize what I mean, wait for the moment when you see again after a cataract operation done expertly with the newest technology. You'll exclaim, 'My God!' That's *brightness* (see *Emptiness and Brightness*).

God. In moving over to a **non-realist** view of God in 1980, I discarded belief in the objective existence of God; but I continued to *believe in* God as a guiding spiritual ideal, a 'leading' idea that focuses and orients the religious life. I also found that when my parents died I loved them and thought of them more than ever, which suggested to me that one can and does continue to love a dead God, as an 'impossible love object'. (See *Impossible Loves*, 2007.)

Incidentally, although there has been much writing about **the Death of God** in the past two centuries, nobody has remarked upon the fact that in Egyptian and some other Bronze-Age religion the God of the dead, though himself dead, yet continued in a sense to live on in the Underworld, where amongst other things he welcomed the dead Pharaoh and helped to maintain the continuity of life above ground. There is thus a similarity between the way my dead God and my dead parents live on together in the same region of my imagination and the way Osiris and the dead Pharaoh lived on in the Underworld and continued to support the state of the world above. In a minimal sense, the dead live on because they still affect us. We think of them sometimes as 'looking down' upon us.

Another example of the paradoxes that surround God's existence or non-existence. Even atheists may describe a particularly desolate area of town or of culture as 'godless'. In such a place, God is 'conspicuous by his absence', as the phrase goes. Jacques Derrida is the modern who has written best about the

42

way in which we are still haunted by our lost God. How long it will go on, we cannot yet say. See **Death etc.**

God, a 'leading' idea. In some recent books I have been trying to state a replacement for Christianity's Grand Narrative theology, a great quasi-historical myth of cosmic Creation, Fall and Redemption. My new story is a theology of the history of religions, which purports to show how it was not God but *religious thought* which slowly dragged us out of our animal background and made us what we are today. For example, I replace 'God created us' with 'the *Idea* of God made us what we are'.

God was the developing role-model: as we aspired after him we were gradually taught by him how we too could be free, conscious, mobile selves, able to use language to order **our world** and to pledge ourselves to act consistently in it. God persuaded us of the possibility of becoming conscious subjects: God was the first I AM. And God showed us how we can convert Chaos into an ordered, unified Cosmos; God persuaded us that it is possible 'to see into someone else's mind' and 'read their thoughts'; and God persuaded us that it is possible to make and to keep promises, vows and covenants. God was also the first *moral* being.

I have argued (rightly or wrongly) that the very first forerunner of the idea of God was the totem animal. Gradually, the sacred world became more elaborate. In the Bronze Age it similarly provided a model for the emergent city state. The Sky Father deals chiefly with law, and lesser attendant divinities deal with agriculture, fertility, metalworking, war and so on. All along, the sacred world was the realm in which we tried out gradually more organized and unified ideas of ourselves, of the state, of the Cosmos and of God. God developed a few steps ahead of us, luring us forward.

Of these four domains – the self, society, the world and God – God was the first to become fully unified, roughly through the development of philosophical theism from Philo Judaeus to Augustine (that is between the first and the fourth centuries AD). The Cosmos arguably at last becomes fully unified during the seventeenth century and the state (perhaps) in people like Frederick the Great. The full unification of the self comes last of all, because it cannot come about until the I–Thou relationship between the self and God has been superseded, by the so-called 'Death' of God that finally sets us free. Perhaps it may be better to re-describe the Death of God as the 'internalization of God'. Giving up his own objective reality, God dies into us and sets us free.

The God who led us at last beyond our ancestral theological realism can still be venerated and loved, just as our own dead parents can be. He and they 'look down' benignly upon us. See *Theology's Strange Return* (2010) and *A New Great Story* (2010). See also **Death of God; Heterologous thinking; Grand Narrative** theology, etc.

'God is a secular humanist'. Secular means pretty much the same as worldly or mundane: of or belonging to this world, the present age and current historical conditions. My slogan is part of a general programme of trying to subvert all the mindless clichés that block religious thought. It means, 'You say that God has become incarnate in Christ. *God from everlasting*, he is now *Man for evermore*. So God has been content to become and to remain human in the world: God is a secular humanist.' From which two conclusions follow. The first is that the popular account of 'secular humanism' as being somehow the diametrical opposite to Christianity is quite wrong. The second is that, because our religious ideas always work as leading ideas, we should draw the conclusion that if God is content to become and remain only human in the world, so should we be. Interestingly, the collect for Good Friday in the English *Book of Common Prayer* (1662) was more than half-way to grasping this. The historic mission of biblical religion was always to point the way to a world in which we humans have at last become ourselves and are able to say Amen to our own transient lives on this earth. As for the popular belief commonly repeated to children, that all or almost all of us go straight to Heaven when we die – that's just pixie-dust, fantasy. Please stop lying to children.

The Highest Good, the Summum Bonum. From Plato and Parmenides onwards it was very commonly the task of **philosophy** to lead the mind upwards towards life's Goal, the highest kind of knowledge, the Summum Bonum, the supreme good for a human being, which was immediate and complete intellectual knowledge of the supremely Real and supremely perfect.

In time, the philosopher became a monk and the Chief End of human life became *Visio Dei*, the vision of God. In the Reformed Catechisms the question: 'What is the chief end of Man?' was answered: 'To know God and enjoy him for ever.'

Throughout 23 centuries or so, the common assumption had been that if we could track down the ultimately Real, it would surely turn out to be and perhaps might *have* to be (a) One and (b) Perfect. At the very beginning of the nineteenth century these assumptions began to be questioned and challenged by Schelling and (especially) Schopenhauer, the effective teacher of people like Thomas Hardy, Nietzsche and Freud. Here is the central nerve of modern atheism. See also **Totum Simul.**

Good show! A key phrase in my **Solar Ethics.** Life is seen as a performance, and one should put on a brave show. The ideal is extravertive and breaks consciously with the old ideal of keeping one's 'interior life' secret. Come out and shine!

Grand Narrative, great Story. 'You are the story you tell about yourself': many societies in the past used to recite ritually a list of the great events and the great deeds through which the nation or church had come into being and had been given its mission. In Israel, the Psalter contains some examples (for example Psalms 105, 106, 136, biblical numbering). In ancient Roman rhetoric, a major speech included a section about the great deeds by which the city had been built and built up. In

Christianity, the Anaphora, the great prayer or 'Canon' of the Mass (though now shrunken in most modern versions) used to tell the same Christian great story as is told in the Creeds – a story gradually developed by various early Christian writers until it reached what the West regards as its classical form in Augustine of Hippo.

Since then, the same Christian grand narrative has remained orthodox. In Luther and Calvin it survived the Reformation unchanged. Calvin even tightened it up, and his followers called it 'The Plan of Salvation'. Its latest major retelling was by the Swiss Reformed theologian Karl Barth (1886–1968), who turned it in a more universalist direction, but retained the warm admiration of Rome.

In 1980 the French philosopher J.-F. Lyotard published *The Postmodern Condition: A Report on Knowledge* (ET, Manchester University Press, 1984), which, very influentially, listed one of the key features of postmodernity as 'scepticism towards Grand Narratives' (*grands récits*). He had in mind all great stories of a long journey towards a final liberation of humanity, but his readers thought chiefly of the Roman Catholic one and of its awkward younger brother, the Marxist one.

I have made half a dozen attempts over the years to write a replacement for the old Grand Narrative, roughly, *very* roughly, along lines adumbrated by Irenaeus and G. W. Lessing: as a story of the education of the human race. Roughly, God didn't create us, but the history of religions did. It was by *religion* that we were first enabled to become conscious, to think our human condition and to struggle painfully out of natural necessities. Religious ideas are, as I have been saying, 'leading' ideas: they give us something to aspire after; they give us the hope that one day we'll do better, much better. As I have said, all the books I have tried to write along these lines have failed. The critics have understandably hated them, but I hope that the ideas are a little clearer and better in the most recent of these many efforts, *A New Great Story* (2010). See also **Autological and Heterological thinking.**

H

Heresy, heretic. From the Greek verb *haereomai* (I choose). A heresy is an opinion that one has worked out for oneself, as opposed to the 'orthodox' opinions laid down by religious authority and accepted by all the obedient faithful. Since philosophers are by their vocation obliged to be free thinkers who acknowledge no other mistress but reason, all philosophers are potential heretics – and most of the great heretics of the early Church were indeed philosopher–theologians. Since the Church decided what books were to survive (it owned the libraries, and it paid for the copying of manuscripts) the great early heretics mostly survive, alas, only in their refutations. One notable exception is John Scotus Erigena (810–77). His book survives, but he himself is said to have been stabbed to death after a lecture by indignant students, who used their steel pens. I have been a little luckier. My worst injury suffered while lecturing was a compound fracture in my left foot. It happened in Beijing in about 2003 and was not caused by the students. They were somewhat surprised, in fact. 'That's not usual!' they said. I finished the lecture.

The alternative to being a philosopher–heretic is to accept some text, or person, or institution as dogmatically authoritative. But the growth of the systematically critical and questioning type of thinking has by now completely demythologized all the old authorities. There is now no credible alternative in religious thought but to be critical, to be a philosopher – in short, we need to revive the ancient idea of the philosopher as a wanderer who all his life seeks to understand the human condition and to get as high as a human can get in pursuit of the **Summum bonum**. We must go back to our beginning and start afresh.

When all this finally became clear in the late nineteenth century, most theologians chose to remain respectable by becoming purely historical theologians. They can advise on what orthodoxy is, and they know their history of ideas, but whether any of it is actually *true* is a question upon which they need not pronounce. This was called 'the flight into history'. It is still customary, so that today the radical or 'creative' theologian is almost the only serious theologian who remains in business.

Heterologous thinking. My neologism for the indirect, mythico-religious, 'Just-So-Story' kind of thinking that was common until the rise of **philosophy** 26 centuries ago and is still very popular. It explains uncomfortable, painful facts of the human condition and hopes to persuade us to accept them as normal. For example: Why do humans speak 8000 different languages? Answer: We once spoke one language and were so strong the gods became jealous, and they scattered us and made us all talk different languages. Sometimes the myths are amusing. Here is an East African cattle nomad's account of men, women and animals: Why is it that the men own all the cattle, but it's the women who have to get up and take them out to pasture in the mornings? Answer: The women once owned huge and varied herds, but they were lazy and failed to get up in the morning. Their animals became impatient, broke free and went off into the wild, leaving the women with no animals. They had to become the servants of men, leading men's cattle out to pasture. And so it is to this day. But look at all those wild beasts out on the plains! The whole of what we call 'the wild' once belonged to women. (Actually, that last thought is rather good.)

Heterologous thinking tells similar stories about the origin of **evil** and the origin of **death**. Once there was no evil, but then first some of the angels fell, and then our first parents fell. Once there was no death: we were created to be naturally immortal, being regularly supplied with fresh skins. But a cunning snake stole our new skins for itself.

Such stories are prominent in Christian doctrine. But today we are at last ready for fully autologous thinking and should stop indulging ourselves by retelling the old tales. See also **Autological and Heterological thinking.**

Heteronomy (Greek: 'by a Law that is *other*'). The state or condition of living under a law externally imposed upon one by social or political or religious authority, or simply of being ruled by one's own passions and so not free. It is generally – and presumably rightly – assumed that early human beings were gradually disciplined by the moral pressure exerted by the groups to which they needed to belong ('the social sanction'), then by customary law administered by tribal chiefs and such, then by formal codes of law promulgated and administered by the sovereign authority in the early state ('the civil sanction'). But both in the Jewish and in the Christian traditions there remains a contrast between a state of pupillage or discipline under which we live now and a state of adult freedom to which we hope one day to graduate. It has generally been thought that we will become fully adult and morally free in the last age of the world when (for example) God puts his own Spirit into our hearts to act as our own conscience. Since the Enlightenment it has generally been claimed that human beings have come of age and are now ready for full autonomy. See **the Autonomy of Religion**. Radical theologians usually seek to internalize God, or in effect to replace him with the ethical teaching and the personal freedom of Jesus. They may quote the book of Revelation to indicate that in the last world (or 'the New Jerusalem') **God** is no longer experienced as a distinct being, but rather is a general and pervasive Brightness.

Etty Hillesum, b.1914 at Middelburg, Holland into a talented Jewish family, died in Auschwitz, 30 November 1943. Her literary remains – enough for one largish volume of diaries and letters – were collected and passed to a writer named Klaas Smelik. His son Klaas A. D. Smelik finally secured the publication of an abridged version of the material in Dutch in 1981 (English 1983). This abridged version is still obtainable, under the title *An Interrupted Life*.

Since then, Etty Hillesum's reputation has slowly grown. Klaas A. D. Smelik is now Director of the Etty Hillesum

Research Centre at Ghent University, which holds the original documents. A complete text finally appeared in Dutch in 1986 and in English in 2002. This last book is out of print as I write, but a second-hand copy can be purchased on the internet.

Early books about Etty Hillesum often seek to appropriate her for some sectarian orthodoxy. For example, they point to her uses of the word 'God', but they fail to notice that she was much influenced by Jungians and all her uses of 'God' are Jungian and non-realistic. But when Etty Hillesum is read more carefully and with greater honesty, I believe that she will be considered one of the most important religious figures of the past 100 years. She is remarkably **solar**. More consistently than almost anyone else in the modern period, she tried to live without **ressentiment** (q. v.). She took Tolstoy and the Bible with her on the train to Auschwitz. Read her, closely.

Humanism. A word which has had many meanings during its lengthy history. It once referred to the culture of ancient Greece and Rome and so to 'human letters' rather than 'sacred letters'. In modern use, it commonly means a world-view which recognizes that:

1. Only man builds a large and complex world around himself, a world that nowadays includes a vast system of scientific theory.
2. In man **the world** became at last conscious of itself as the world of man, *our* **world**.
3. In this perception of the world as *our* world that belongs to us, there is a modern Return of ancient ideas of a sovereign cosmic human that are to be found in almost all the great religions. (See *Theology's Strange Return*, Appendix on Humanism). I argue that Christianity in particular was always going to evolve into humanism.

Notice what an interesting price the world has to pay, in order to become conscious of itself. It does become conscious, but only in and through our appropriation of it. In our appropriation of it, it acquires its dazzling brightness. It glows demurely, like an old-fashioned pre-feminist wife, but it can identify itself only via the husband to whom it belongs. There is here some Return of the old-fashioned Christian and Marxist idea of 'man's sovereignty over nature': all things are yours, says Saint Paul. But in its 'Returned' version this idea now comes with the corollary that we alone are responsible for our own world-picture and for our collective management of our world.

See also the following entries on **The Human Lifeworld** etc.

The Human Lifeworld, its primacy and centrality. The term 'lifeworld' (*Lebenswelt*) was introduced by Edmund Husserl (1859–1938), who started his philosophy with human subjective consciousness, the world of everyday human life being its first object. A good indication of the way we have moved over by now to the human-centred viewpoint is the way we have now come to speak *not* of 'natural rights', but of *'human* rights'. They're not 'natural' (is anything?): they are human historical creations.

If we start strictly within *our world*, how do we ever get into *the* objective world? We don't: it's obvious that once we have understood that we are always in *our* world, we must recognize that we cannot get across to the purely objective standpoint of *the* world. So I have often said that in effect, only **our world** exists. But since in practice we need to be able to say that some news reports and some histories are more 'objective' than others, we need objective reality and objective truth as 'Regulative Ideas' in Kant's sense – professional ideals for journalists and historians to be guided by. Never actually realized, but ethically productive and valuable.

Thus by the mid-1980s I had extended my **non-realism** from God to the World and even (you may already have noticed) to the Mind. The old Aristotelean realism of the later Middle Ages is replaced by various kinds of constructivism.

See **Fact and Interpretation:** all this is a familiar trope both in British Empiricist philosophy after Locke and also in Nietzsche's philosophy. I like nihilism: it's a liberation. The old sceptics called it *ataraxia*, a serenely uncommitted habit of mind. Puzzling when we first meet it and hard to learn: but when we get there, it works.

Human realism. Once we have accepted that we are always inside ourselves and our own point of view, that only we *have* a world-view at all and that we have no access to any absolute vision of the world against which we can check our own view, we realize that 'From now on we are on our own', without any higher tribunal or court of appeal. The only world we can know is always already a *human* world.

Many philosophers, including two great figures who are still with us, Putnam and Dummett, will broadly accept this **anti-realist** view. But both they and I will want to acknowledge that for everyday practical purposes it's perfectly reasonable to go along with the current consensus world-picture. It's only human, but like *Wikipedia* it gets so much democratic tweaking and amending that it ends up by being quite good enough for most of us, most of the time. In that respect, it resembles Newtonian physics, another world we have left behind but can still fall back upon harmlessly.

This undogmatic acceptance of the objectivity of our knowledge for practical purposes I often call human realism. See the long article **Realism, etc.**

Humanitarian ethics. A humanitarian was at first, in the early nineteenth century, a person who in doctrine particularly stressed the humanity of Jesus. From the 1840s or so it came to mean a 'philanthropist', a person who puts universal love for the fellow human being, and especially for unfortunates, first in ethics.

An ancient Roman writer declares *nihil humanum a me alienum puto* ('I deem nothing human alien to myself'), but he probably owned slaves. The most universally loved early humanist is the Jesus of Saint Luke's Gospel. Britain, land of a million charities, has had a strong 'voluntary sector' since Norman times and pioneered new humanitarian foundations in great numbers from the 1730s onward. Right-wing factory owners, like the old landed aristocracy before them, long tended to fight against decent pay, conditions and human rights for their workers, but in the modern period since the 1960s the standing of the world 'humanitarian' in the language has become unassailable. Long may it remain so!

In this radical **humanism/humanitarianism** I see a modern return of the first-millennium picture of Christ in Majesty, ruling over the world. See *Theology's Strange Return*.

I

Identity. As part of the 2011 UK national census, people who received the official form were invited (not *ordered* by law, because the whole topic is so sensitive) – 'invited', then to define themselves in terms of their 'identity', whether ethnic, or national, or religious. There were many options to choose from, too many.

The question turned out to be very difficult even to *phrase* in a way acceptable to all the people who had the form to fill in. If the question was 'What's your *race*?', there would be all sorts of problems. The Jews are not a 'race' in the sense recognized by anthropologists. Nor are 'coloureds', 'darkies', or 'blacks' or whatever. After extensive interbreeding the definition of 'black' gets hopelessly vague. How black do you have to be to be 'black'? The question about nationality, 'Where are you from?', is equally confusing. Your parents may still wear the old national dress, eat the old food, use the old language and look to the ambassador of the country they came from for protection; but you were born here and see no reason to call yourself anything but British, which is what you've always been from birth. As for the question about religion, if you are at all

53

politically and culturally aware, you may very well choose to define your identity in religious terms. 'I'm a Muslim', you say – but today that may be said by someone who comes from almost anywhere in the world. There are over a billion Muslims and they are very varied; but whether you are from Morocco or from Bangladesh, whatever country has issued your passport, and whatever your precise shade of olive or brown, you'll probably say insistently: 'I don't want to say anything more about my "identity" except that I'm a Muslim.'

One conclusion the unfortunate civil servants who drew up the Census form agreed upon was this: more people now want to define their identity in religious terms. And that applies, not only to Muslims and Jews, but also to Christians. Think of all those countries around and south of the Sahara where the Northern half of the country is predominantly Muslim, and the Southern half is predominantly Christian. Once the Northerners start calling themselves Muslim and making demands, the Southerners are likely to do the same and therefore start calling themselves Christians.

Now think of other cases around the world. Of Unionist working people in Northern Ireland who are really only *culturally* 'Protestants' now; of Tamils in Sri Lanka who call themselves Hindus, perhaps in the hope of getting more sympathy and support from India; of the large Tibetan community – religious, ethnic, national? – in north India and so on. We can now draw a few conclusions:

There is a great deal of identity-politics in the modern world, as a result of globalization, the mass migration of workers and their families and their fear of assimilation. People are clutching at almost anything that will serve as a communal badge of *identity* for them – even something like: 'We are travelling people' – but very often it is *religion* that makes the most convenient, conspicuous and durable badge. And amongst Christians, although over much of the world Christianity the religion is in decline, the number of people who want to *call* themselves Christian is actually increasing.

In brief, the more I think about 'identity', the less I like it. I prefer anonymity and globalization. Especially I admire the international aid worker, who sets aside any national insignia and becomes simply a UN agent. Most particularly, I deplore the 'heritagization' of religion and its increasing use as a badge of identity in places where there is intercommunal strife. We should have nothing to do with anything of that kind, for it simply exacerbates conflict. I disclaim identity, and that is one more reason for talking about empty radical **humanism** (q. v.).

Impossible Loves. All of us experience curiously strong yearnings after objects that cannot possibly be attained by us. We still feel this impossible love for the dead (especially our dead parents), for the dead God, for the old faith that we have lost, for lost youth, lost innocence, lost ideals, for chances that we missed because we failed to seize them while the 'window of opportunity' was open and for all the other lives and other loves that might have been ours.

Such impossible, quasi-religious yearnings play a large part in our imaginative lives nowadays. Why? In the days when faith in the divine Predestination of all events was strong there was only one way things could go and that was the way they actually went. You were not encouraged to daydream about other possible lives you might have lived. Today, however, my actual self is only one amongst many possibilities. The best cure for too much languishing is to be *solar*, to live to its fullest the one life we actually have and to learn to say a full Amen to one's own and only life.

Inside out. Perhaps it is some kind of character-fault in me, but I have a curious habit of wanting to invert or turn inside out almost every received doctrine or saying that presents itself. In spirituality, I reject the traditional move into one's own inwardness and instead say that we should live by 'outing' ourselves all the time. This movement outwards is literally an 'e/motion'. Maybe it's because we live in revolutionary times, when many people feel the need for a 'revaluation of all values', a reversal of everything.

Internalization. If you were to visit the South Pole, would it look in any way different from everywhere else for hundreds of miles around? If you look over the side of your ship as it crosses the Equator, will you see a black line running across the sea? No. The South Pole and the Equator don't actually exist out there. They are, both of them, features of a mathematical grid that we impose upon the world. We can use the grid of lines of latitude and longitude to specify places exactly. Shorelines and the courses of rivers move, but the grid is fixed – not because it's real, but because it is conceptual.

During the past two or three centuries a whole lot of cultural material that we used to think of as existing out there has come instead to be seen as stuff in our heads with which we build and interpret our world. The imagination, which used to be suspect because Satan attacked us through it, is now valued much more highly. It is *creative*. The human mind is not just a blank slate, or wax tablet, upon which nature impresses our experience. No, the human mind is actively creative; it's a natural world-builder. It must sally forth and *make sense* of the world. Scientists don't just 'discover' the laws of nature. They *invent* them and then show how they can usefully be applied to the data to make successful forecasts.

Notice a little paradox that may confuse you. When we talk about internalization, we seem to be concentrating everything within the self. For example, people may say: 'They used to believe in demons who might get into your head and possess you; and they did a lot of exorcizing to get rid of those demons. But today we'd describe the whole thing in psychological terms. The demons were just forbidden wishes, tempting us, and such things as that.'

So far as it goes, that's fair enough. But we need to say a little more: 'It's true that a great deal of stuff that we used to think of as nature and as existing out there, we should now regard as being part of our ideal culture and as internal to the self. Very well, but it's not just a matter of allowing the self to become bigger and fatter. What we now need to do is to reverse the direction of movement and say, 'The ideal culture in our heads gives us a huge repertoire of symbolic forms that help us to get our feelings out into productive **expression**, so enabling us to get ourselves together and to build a richer and more valuable world around ourselves.'

Don't see the long process of *internalization* as being *opposed* to the newer expressivist idea of the self. No: the long process of internalization has enriched our idea of the self and its creativity, enabling us to recognize how human beings are all the time actively making and remaking their own worlds.

The Interpretative Plasticity of the World. A phrase from as far back as *The Leap of Reason* (1976). I very early accepted that there isn't just one correct theory and description of **the world**. There will always be the possibility of a new theory, a fresh angle, a different description. So we should learn to do without the idea of a single real and final **Truth** of things, stated in some final language. No: we seem to be stuck with pluralism, and I for one prefer it.

J

The Jesus of History and the Christ of Faith. From early times people have remarked upon a certain duality in the figure of Jesus. First there was the contrast between the man seen by the welcoming crowds and the dangerous heretic and blasphemer seen by Jesus' enemies. Then there was the contrast between the earthly Jesus, an 'ugly little man', and the risen and glorified Jesus, who is always pictured as looking like a Greek god. Then there was the contrast between the Jewish teacher of Matthew, Mark and Luke and the Jesus of Saint John, 'the spiritual Gospel', whose talk and actions are very

57

different. Finally, in the early Church, there was the formally defined Two-Natures doctrine, which according to the Bishop of Rome, Leo I, writing in 449, has the earthly Jesus switching his costume from Clark Kent in a business suit to Superman: sometimes he acts in and through his human nature and behaves just like any other man, and at other times he acts in and through his divine nature and performs mighty works.

These early ideas about Jesus were crystallized in the 'Two Natures, One Person' doctrine defined in 451 at the Council of Chalcedon. In the Incarnate Lord two complete Natures, Human and Divine, are conjoined without confusion in the One Person of God's co-equally divine Son. The question of whether such a dogma could be made psychologically plausible was postponed until critical-historical research came along. Then, in the new era of historical novel-writing, people began to ask themselves what it might have been like to be Jesus. Does the hesitant, rather reticent Clark Kent really know all the time that he's a figure with superhero powers? Did a first-century builder's son really *know* that he is God Almighty?

These questions came to a head in David Friedrich Strauss's *The Life of Jesus Critically Examined* (1835/6), which clearly indicated that the original Jesus was just a human teacher and healer, who after his death had been elaborately mythicized by his followers over a long period. Once stated, this thesis was unignorable, but from the later Schleiermacher to the present day there have been mildly liberal but doctrinally conservative theologians who have tried to argue that the Christ of dogma is a slowly developed, but God-guided and basically correct interpretation of the original Jesus. Strauss in his later years attacked that thesis in his *The Christ of Faith and the Jesus of History* (1865).

This duality, between the man and the myth, has become a permanent fact to be reckoned with. The main effort to overcome it has been made by people who postulated that in becoming incarnate the divine Son voluntarily set aside, or emptied himself of, or became voluntarily unaware of his own divine attributes. Such theories of *kenosis* or self-emptying may be philosophically absurd, but they do show modern **humanism** wanting to be able to imagine what it must have been like to be Jesus.

There remains to be mentioned another and even more challenging duality. In the New Testament, in Early Christian thought, and in Christian art much is made of Jesus as the obedient Son of God, nailed to the Father's Will. But throughout we also hear of another verdict upon Jesus – that he really *was* a rebel and blasphemer who came to destroy the divine Law – and we hear also of another, rebellious Son of God, or Morning Star, who (when both of them are seen in their glorified state) is iconographically indistinguishable from Jesus. Evidently the Church's religion of obedience to the Will of the Father, with Jesus as our role-model, has another religion behind it and kept largely out of sight. See **Lucifer.**

K

Kingdom-religion, Kingdom theology. Among certain of the French Catholic Modernists there was a saying to the effect that: 'Jesus preached the Kingdom, but what we got was the Church' – a fairly savage remark, if you recall that for them 'the Church' was a huge, musty, creaking power-structure centred in Rome, a 'system' that was to crush them all.

In Jesus' teaching the longed-for utopian society at the End of the World, the Kingdom, was a new moral order, a new order of human relationships in which there would be no **ressentiment**, no negative feelings. People would live in a spirit of pure generosity: they would love even their enemies. And this new world would come when people decided for it. The rabbis had often said that the promised time would come when people fully obeyed the Law, but Jesus went further in calling for an excessive, 'solar' generosity of spirit. He does not seem to have envisaged any continuation of organized religion, with its elaborately graded hierarchy of expensive professionals and its complex mediation between the individual human and God. None of that would be needed any more, after God had become fully dispersed into people. 'I saw no Temple in the City,' says the writer of Revelation (21.22).

So the Church arose as a night-watchman, a temporary formation filling the gap until Jesus returned and the new age began. On the far left of the Reformation some groups did think that the ecclesiastical period was now ended, and it was up to them now to generate religious societies of the new 'Kingdom' type. Of them the most notable survivor is the Society of Friends, the Quakers.

In modern times many liberal Anglicans have been attracted to Quakerism. The prolific early-Victorian theologian F. D. Maurice (1805–72) wrote *The Kingdom of Christ, or Hints to a Quaker . . .* (1838), by way of explaining that although much attracted to Quakerism, he had decided to stay with the Church.

He might think differently today. Traditional Church-Christianity took for granted the absolute monarchy of God in Heaven and of the King (or Tsar or Emperor) on earth. When political democracy arrives on earth, decentring political power and dispersing it through the entire electorate, surely it must be obvious that the time has come to democratize Christianity too, by going Quakerish and post-ecclesiastical.

My friend David Boulton (author of *The Trouble with God* and *Who on Earth was Jesus?*), being himself a 'Quaker humanist' and close to me in religious outlook, would much prefer to use the phrase 'The Republic of Heaven' to describe the Kingdom. He's probably right, but I feel that we are still suspended between two epochs, both in Church and in State, so that in the short run the old biblical language is probably clearest. I have been advocating a changeover to 'Kingdom'-type theology and religion at least since *Radicals and the Future of the Church* (1989).

Postscript: In May 2011 I received a copy of a leaflet headed: 'Introducing the Non-Theist Friends Network', and reporting that a significant number of people have already joined the first explicitly non-theistic group within one of Britain's historical religious denominations. The Friends, or Quakers, do of course already have a somewhat demythologized conception of God, and there has for some years been a Quaker Universalist group; but this further step is a portent and remarkable.

L

Landscape Art, Eastern and Western. To illustrate the difference between my ultralite or **featherlite** vision of the world, and the one that is or rather, *was* more typical of the West, I often point to the difference between Oriental and Western landscape painting. The Western landscape is typically much richer and more weighted by gravity toward the bottom of the composition, because our Creator has made it and has set it firmly and foursquare on solid foundations. Abundant birds and beasts speak of Eden. But the reminder of Eden creates an air of nostalgia and guilt over the ancient sin that caused us to lose all this. Finally, the Western landscape painting from Rubens onwards very often says: 'This is my property'.

The best Eastern landscapes, Chinese or Japanese, are not anybody's property. This is the floating world, featherlite and not freighted down by anything. They delicately describe or evoke the fleeting beauty of impermanence, especially in the common stress on the seasons and the weather. This is transience experienced as pure beauty and quite untainted by the Western sense of ancestral loss.

Once you have learnt to appreciate Oriental landscape, don't you prefer it? And is it not now clear to you that all that Western *realism*, that solid sense of the world's melancholy sunset magnificence, was merely an ideological effect, produced by a lot of theology we no longer believe in?

If you disagree with me, do please at least take a good look at Hiroshige, Hokusai and Utamaro.

Language is only about itself, Language is much cleverer than the people who speak it, Language speaks us, Let language do the talking. Through slogans like these I attempted to introduce some typically postmodern ideas about language.

The first slogan goes back to Friedrich von Schiller (1759–1805) and makes a point that I have made by quoting a one-language dictionary. To use the book you must already be within the language, within the book every word's meaning is described only by other words, and there is no way out of the book. The system, complex, living and in slow, ceaseless change, is not in any visible way hooked on to anything *non-*linguistic and outside it. The meaning of any individual word is not a thing on the other side of it that it *stands for*; no, the meaning of a word is given by the way it is used and the jobs it does along with other words in the daily circulation of our language. All meaning is historically changeable, relativistic and shifting: but it has to be so in order to allow historical change.

All this began to be understood in the great creative period when Germany stirred at the end of the eighteenth century, but the full implications were not spelt out for over a century. When I'm born and learn my native language, I am inducted into a **human lifeworld** in which I can communicate and interact with others. Because the living language is so much bigger and older than me, it often seems to be smarter than me – especially when I make a Freudian slip, or speak with unconscious irony. In my own work I have 'thought' by trying to listen to language free-running and citing slogans like 'Let language do the talking' and 'Language speaks us'.

In this context, note that, for the same reason that I write being as **be-ing**, the participle, I should really write meaning as **mean-ing**, a process, *semeiosis*, signifying a process that takes time. For example, a sentence has not delivered its meaning in full until it has been uttered in full – and perhaps not even then. It looks as if meaning, like consciousness, always arrives a bit late.

It was thoughts like these that finally drove out of my head the notion that God is a language-user, who speaks to people. The more we study it, the more we come to see that a living language is completely embedded in a people's social life in time. How *can* an eternal Being be thought of as uttering or even understanding a sentence? Can the eternal Absolute Being be thought of as one amongst others in a social world whose denizens *need* language? Obviously not. See also **Analogy**.

The Leap of Reason (1976). As early as 1960 or so, in a collaboration with a friend (see *Theology's Strange Return*, 2010, p. 101), I first raised the question of whether a person brought up inside a completely self-contained and closed world could be imagined as one day conceiving the possibility of an Outside to all this. Could this character begin to describe 'Outside', and could he fill out the idea and give it some positive content? At least, it is a highly consciousness-raising idea. The *Leap of Reason*, a variant of Kierkegaard's leap of faith, shows me still attempting an approach to God through metaphysics: but like the Oxford theologian Austin Farrer I was already replacing rational *argument* with a rational *intuition*. A bad sign.

At that age I was still far too young to be able to take these thoughts any further. In **philosophy** especially, one scarcely even *begins* to understand the subject until one has been teaching it at university level for many years. (Newspapers think that universities exist to teach undergraduates: in fact, their most useful effect is the gradual education of the dons, or some of them.) By 1973 I was 39 and just about old enough to attempt the book; but it wasn't published till 1976. And I now cordially disapprove of any appeal in philosophy to leaps and intuitions.

Life, The Religion of Ordinary Life. During the late 1990s I was wondering whether to build my religious philosophy around Heidegger's notion of Being, or around the idea of ordinary everyday life. Or perhaps around the Sun and being 'solar'.

At that time I was thinking a great deal about ordinary language, like the novelist Angus Wilson, who admitted to sitting behind gossips on the bus with pencil and notebook, recording their speech. I was picking out and collecting philosophically interesting new phrases. I wrote down hundreds, but when I did a count it was apparent that 'life' was the winner. Even in nineteenth-century literature it was already obvious that many people, on losing their belief in God and the supernatural world, were instead turning to life as the new religious object. *Not* the mechanistic universe and the new even more mechanistic technology, and *not* just 'the economy'. Nor was the new religion of Art, espoused by the aesthetes, a satisfactory replacement for God. No: after considering these options, many Victorians such as John Ruskin began a process of investing life, just life, just everyday human social life in this world, with a new kind of sanctity and dignity.

Within the British tradition a tendency to sacralize ordinary domestic life goes back at least to the seventeenth century, to the hymns of Bishop Cosin and George Herbert and to the Dutch painters. In the modern period it became very strong in influential writers like D. H. Lawrence and F. R. Leavis. But the big explosion of new life-idioms in common speech began during or just after the Second World War. (I recently noted *We have a duty to life* in a Second World War film.) By the time I became interested in them, there were hundreds of life idioms, they were very varied, and it had become easy to make a point familiar to students of Feuerbach and Nietzsche: long ago culture had asset-stripped the world of everyday and domestic life in order to enrich the supernatural world. But now the process of secularization was bringing all that prodigious wealth back down into the everyday world from which it had been stolen. The result was an astonishing revaluation –

even a *sacralization* – of life. *Life, Life* (2003) lists some 250 idioms. Its title is a double quotation, from the opening of *The Pilgrim's Progress* and from the poet Harold Monro.

Interestingly, although Christianity was for far too long dominated by an anti-life mentality, Judaism has always been more pro-life, from the Bible ('The LORD is the strength of my life', Psalm 27.1) to the present day. When toasting, gentiles commonly drink to someone's good health: the Jews drink 'To life'.

Life's a Package Deal. The recent shift in the West, away from our traditional God-centred and other worldly outlook and towards a popular religion of ordinary life in this world, is very evident in our new idioms which speak of the 'sanctity' of marriage, of the home, of family life, of a person's privacy and even of bird sanctuaries and primal wildernesses. It has also suddenly and very strikingly changed our attitude to 'the Problem of **Evil**'.

The traditional first-millennium God was absolutely perfect, unmixed in his goodness and holiness and purity. Compared with God, this miserable world of ours was so unstable and corrupt that the only rational course was to renounce it and embrace 'the religious life' of a celibate monk or nun. A sincere theist must reject this world. The noblest, truest answer to the Problem of Evil was to become a hermit, or an anchorite, who rejects the world and lives for God alone.

Life is quite unlike God as a religious object. It is capacious, even baggy and includes every degree of good and evil, fortune and misfortune, comedy and tragedy. If we are going to 'choose life' – as, in a sense, most of the Jews have always done – then we have to accept it, warts and all, as a package deal that cannot be renegotiated. There is no point in trying to *blame* life for being unfair. The birds and woodland animals in Janáček's opera live very short, very hard lives; but they affirm even their own brief lives with a kind of frantic joy. Why cannot *we* do that? We have at least the advantage that we can do, and in places have already done, a great deal to make life better for ourselves and for others.

So in the religion of life we do not flee from the world like the monks. We affirm life, plunging into **the Fray**, trying to live life to its fullest and trying to love life and all that lives with as much uninhibited generosity and freedom from **ressentiment** as we can muster. By being **solar** we try to overcome evil with love and to say a sincere Amen to our own lives, including our own disasters.

I pose then a dilemma: if you want to affirm the traditional absolutely pure, holy and perfect God, you must be consistently world-renouncing. You must withdraw from the world into silence and solitude and seek by various mortifications to fit yourself to meet your Maker.

Alternatively, accept that life is a package deal, dismiss the 'Problem of Evil' and plunge into **the Fray**. Try to **make the most of it**.

You may say that my dilemma leaves out the option chosen by religion since the late Middle Ages – namely the attempt to affirm *both* the traditional realist Heavenly Father *and* this world. But that modern attempt to make the old otherworldly celibate religion into a world-affirming faith has failed. It was soon found to make the Problem of Evil both very urgent and theoretically insoluble. That is one of the main reasons why we have radical theology.

We live along the wires, etc. See **Language is only about itself**, above.

Lost in the objectivity of world-love. My emotive-expressive view of personal life – the actual living that each of us does every day – is that it consists in a continuous, many-stranded outpouring of feeling that comes up out of us, gets coded into language and other forms of symbolic expression and is then spread out over the common human life world, which is thereby invested with meaning and value.

This coming-out into **expression,** in which all our life consists, is also a going-out into 'objectivity' or death. When we are most fully engaged with life we feel very intense absorption and love. Hence the phrase 'lost in the objectivity of world-love', from *Solar Ethics*. It is the self's living-by-dying-all-the-time and I attribute the same everliving, ever-dying life to 'God' in the sense of the Whole. Our pouring-out and passing away into objectivity is part of a universal joyous pouring out and passing away. That's *Comment c'est*, How it goes.

The use of 'objectivity' to mean 'death', as I complete the process of expressing myself, comes from Georges Bataille. Notice that in all this discussion I am battling against the tendency to think of **Death** and **Life** as two distinct and opposite powers or states. On the contrary, being is always transient and living is therefore always dying.

Lucifer is, in Latin, 'the light-bringer'. In Greek the equivalent word is Phōsphoros, the name of an element so unstable that it glows in the dark and ignites spontaneously. Being so unstable, and therefore a 'base' element, makes Phōsphoros a good name for Satan.

Behind the name Lucifer is a long and curious story. The planet Venus, being so much closer to the Sun than Earth is, often rises in the East just before dawn and appears in the West just as the Sun is setting. In pre-scientific times the morning appearance of Venus was named Lucifer, the Morning Star, and its evening appearance was called Hesperus, the Evening Star. In the Bible, not only the Morning Star, but a number of other stars too, might appear just before sun-up. Collectively, they may be thought of as 'the morning stars', or even as the 'sons of God', for example in Job 38.7. 'Where were you', asks God, on the first morning of creation . . .

When the morning stars sang together,
And all the sons of God shouted for joy?

Thus the rising Sun and its attendant stars were a natural symbol of God, surrounded by his heavenly court of 'ministers' or 'angels'.

67

Around these phenomena grew up a very potent myth referred to by the prophet Isaiah (14.12–15):

How are you fallen from heaven
  O Day Star, son of Dawn! . . .
You said in your heart,
  'I will ascend to heaven;
Above the stars of God
  I will set my throne on high; . . .
But you are brought down to Sheol (= Hell, or the Underworld)
  To the depths of the Pit.

Here is the origin of at least the first episodes in the fully developed Myth of Satan. He had begun life as the first and greatest of God's creatures. But the best and brightest of the Sons of the Morning had rebelled against the divine order. In his vanity he had tried to usurp the place of God, and a number of other angels had joined him. But when God arose in his full strength Lucifer and his allies were quickly eclipsed and cast down from Heaven. By this stupendous fall a new world came into being, namely Hell, the permanent domain of Satan and the rest of his band of rebel angels. They were fixed at the opposite pole of the Universe from God, but had some power to visit Earth in order to test and to tempt humans. They entered us via the imagination, the faculty in us that can be troubled by sinful thoughts.

Lucifer began as a very beautiful, golden-haired, heavenly being who looked like a Greek god; but the fallen Lucifer, Satan, was usually portrayed as a hideous monster until the late Middle Ages when, in the *Très Riches Heures* of Le Duc de Berry, he is first portrayed as a beautiful man, crowned and robed, in his glorious aspect. This seems to be the beginning of a long process of rehabilitation, especially when the gradual rise of modern democratic politics begins to make Satan a more sympathetic figure.

In all the seven or so primary civilizations, it seems that power and authority came down from the gods through those who ruled on their behalf. Some form of monarchy was the norm. Even as late as Victorian times, children learnt that there were animal, vegetable and mineral 'kingdoms'. There were – I think, still *are* – 'noble' and 'base' metals and gases. The lion was the king of beasts, the eagle of birds and the oak of trees. The entire universe in every part of it exhibited a divine order, and you were instructed to know and to keep to your 'place' or 'station' within it. To rebel against it was the greatest sin of all. There were, of course, some popular uprisings in the later Middle Ages, but they did not have a complete alternative world-view to offer. All they could do was to appeal from the bad king to the good king, and they failed. Even Luther was still so embedded in the old hierarchical world-view that he did not for a moment endorse the politics of the more radical reformers. On the contrary, he supported their savage repression.

John Milton was in a more personally embarrassing position. By his time the Reformation had gone somewhat further. Milton had supported the Parliamentarians: he had been an apologist for regicide. Wasn't he *himself* a rebel against the divine order of things? And yet, in the 1660s, he is dictating the greatest Christian epic poem since Dante, *Paradise Lost*, and he is going to tell the story of the Fall of the Rebel Angels, of the Creation of Man and of the fall of Man, all in such a way as to *confirm* the divine order and justify the ways of God with Man. To do this he must write epic lines in which he must make Lucifer's revolt against God intelligible, without appearing to be *himself* in the least sympathetic to Lucifer's cause.

You don't need to be Derrida to be able to spot Milton's difficulties. They were obvious enough to William Empson and indeed to William Blake, who pronounced very sagely that Milton 'was of the Devil's party without knowing it'. But Blake is *himself* in the same position! His Lucifer is iconographically indistinguishable from the figure of the risen and ascended Christ, who in Revelation proclaims *himself* 'the bright morning star' (22.16). Odder, Jesus also promises to 'give the morning star' to the one who chooses and stays with the right side in the controversies at Thyatira (Revelation 2.28). This suggests that the modern difficulties about the relations between God, Christ and Satan, although they have been exposed by political change, have an origin that goes back deep into the New Testament itself. We need first a brief summary of the strange pattern of resemblances, reversals and contrasts that links the two great and closely intertwined figures of Christ and Satan.

1. Christ is the (only-begotten and eternal) Son of God, whereas Lucifer is the greatest of the (created) Sons of God.

2. Christ in his glorious aspect looks just like Lucifer in his glorious aspect.

3. Both Christ and Lucifer are the Morning Star.

4. Christ in his humiliated and lowly aspect is always fully human; whereas the humiliated Lucifer is for long a hideous monster and begins to look more human again only in early-modern times. Eventually, he is even a gentleman.

5. Both come down from the Heavens to Earth like a bolt of lightning. Jesus 'will baptize you with fire', and he came 'to cast fire upon the earth', lightning having long been seen as a major sign from heaven. Jesus himself declares that in a vision he saw 'Satan fall like lightning from Heaven' (Luke 10.18).

6. Jesus (in the developed theology) is always the seriously tempted but *obedient* Son of God; whereas Satan is always the *rebellious* Son of God. Satan cannot be thought of as changing sides until modern Universalism comes along.

7. Satan is the present ruler of this world, and Jesus the Messiah-designate is the future ruler of this world.

8. Both Satan and Jesus must bear a heavy punishment for the sin of rebellion against God. Indeed Calvin thought

they bore the *same* dreadful damnation; but Satan bore it on his own account, whereas Jesus bore it for us.

9. During his earthly ministry Jesus is regularly charged with blasphemy and with being able to cast out devils only because he is personally in league with the greatest of them all, Beelzebub.

10. Both Lucifer and Jesus have visited all three cosmic realms, Heaven, Earth and Hell, whether as living there by right, or as visiting for business purposes.

This whole story, in its developed Western form, is a great myth of the long war between good and **evil**. But from the first it has contrary undercurrents which suggest that it's a cover-up job. The original Jesus, an ethical teacher standing at the end of the world who pictured a new moral order based *not* on the Law of the Father, but on pure love, seemed to be announcing the end of the Divine Order in the cosmos and the end of the government of human life by divine Law. This was too much for his contemporaries to accept. The 'bad', rebellious and radical-humanist side of Jesus, whose enemies correctly described him as a blasphemer who had prophesied against the Temple and who would destroy the Law, was split off and ascribed to Lucifer. From what was left a new obedient Jesus was constructed, an ecclesiastical Jesus who was a model of passive submission to the will of the Father. Thus God could remain undisturbed in heaven for many centuries.

Out of the very complex materials available, the Christian Fathers gradually assembled the Latin **Grand Narrative** which tells of a long cosmic battle between good and evil – a story that worked pretty well until early-modern times, when the rise of a new democratic sentiment and of a longing for human autonomy began to blow it apart. A partial humanization and even rehabilitation of figures like Lucifer and Judas began, while at the same time there has also long been a desire for a less weak, passive and effeminate image of Jesus himself. I am not suggesting that the disobedient Son of

God and the obedient should simply change places, but rather that the received ecclesiastical Jesus is far too weak a figure to have been the author of the best of the teaching credited to him. Meanwhile, we must await the theologian who can attempt a major deconstruction of the entire Latin Christian Grand Narrative.

M

Make out, make, believe, make sense, making the most of It. Since the 1980s I have used slogans including the verb *to make* by way of emphasizing the roots in ordinary language of my constructivism. In an obvious sense, we ourselves are the makers of the objects of our own knowledge and of our own religious faith.

You're in a field, and sixty or seventy yards away there is a brown tussock. What is it? You screw up your eyes. Can it be a rabbit? Can you see it *as* a rabbit? Yes, you can just make out that it is a rabbit. So what's happened? When you tried to impose the word 'rabbit' upon your rather hazy visual experience of brown, it seemed almost to focus your vision a little more sharply, and your hypothesis seemed to succeed. However, the making out isn't always vindicated. You may walk over to the spot and find that it was indeed only a tussock after all. 'Funny: *I could have sworn* that it was a rabbit.' We do this very rapid framing and testing of visual hypotheses all the time. In the case quoted, a psychologist would have said that 'rabbit!' was an 'object-hypothesis'.

Objects of faith are rather different – partly because when we are in a devout mood we allow our normally habitual self-criticism to lapse. At midnight Mass on Christmas Eve with the candles, the ritual, the music, the familiar words and the crowding memories we forget that ordinarily we are well aware that everything that is happening here is human, with an ascertainable – indeed, mostly very well-known and quite recent – human history. The phrase **make, believe** means 'don't be reluctant to admit that we ourselves are the makers of the objects of our own religious faith. Get on with it!' It's not difficult for a person recently widowed to recognize that she mustn't languish. She must create objects of concern and around them build a meaningful new life. She must join a club, get out more, see some old friends again, do something worthwhile as a volunteer, buy a dog so that it can take her for walks. She may smile at her own weakness, but *of course* we are in the position of knowing that it is up to us to make our own lives 'meaningful'. And that is as true of religion as of everything else, if not more so, because of the great power of religious symbolism to help us make sense of life.

Notice here the *non-cognitivist* implications: I'm saying that faith, the *practice* of religion, is a way of making life make sense. It doesn't have to be objectively true, and indeed, in an obvious sense it is not. But it is a uniquely powerful way of making one's own life make sense, which is why people try out religion for themselves, to see if it works for them. When we feel the need of it, we are perfectly entitled to make the most of It – and that last phrase is really wonderful!

Finally, work out for yourself the same points in connection with the Latin verb *construere*, to assemble materials to build. Hence *construction*, the business of building. Hence also *construing* the structure of a sentence; *construal*, interpretation; and *putting a construction upon . . .*, trying out an interpretation. Now we see the philosophical wealth that is available to us all in our own language.

Meaning, mean-ing. A difficult word with a wide range of uses. Somebody's meaning may be just her *intention*. In other contexts meaning may be *import, significance*, or it may just imply a causal connection, as when dark clouds *mean* that it will rain. Even woollier, people talk of meaning as some sort of soul-satisfying stuff that they are searching for, and of course they talk about *the meaning of life* – perhaps while simultaneously mocking themselves for using such language.

Because of all this fluff, philosophers often prefer to re-strict their own use of the word 'meaning' to linguistic mean-ing. If we start with Wittgenstein's question, 'What is the meaning of a word?', then the likely first move is to describe *English literalism*, the view that a word's meaning is what it stands for and that a fact-stating sentence is a kind of picture or diagram of a state of affairs. People who take this old view of meaning go on to assert that there is such a thing as literal truth. Having explored the limitations of this literal-istic 'picture theory of meaning', Wittgenstein himself then went on to develop his theory of meaning as use. Look at the job the words are being used to do. A conversation is often like a game, and utterances are like moves in a game, as the 'ball' – that is, the initiative – passes from one person to another.

After Wittgenstein, we can hardly fail to recognize that not all words are nouns (Latin: *nomina*, names) and that not all utterances are fact-stating. On the contrary, religious lan-guage is very varied and does a great variety of jobs. For ex-ample, religious language is very highly self-involving: using it, the speaker commits himself, worships, repents, vows. By contrast, scientific language is very general and the ob-server, though always presupposed, is very neutral and non-committal. He might be anybody, and that is the point, whereas in religious utterance you speak for yourself.

I sometimes use **mean-ing** to make the point that language is temporal. Even in a written sentence, there has to be suc-cession, because a change in the word-order may completely change the *force* of a sentence. So mean-ing is temporal, and it always arrives late, in that I only grasp what you are *getting at*, or *driving at*, when your utterance is complete.

Sometimes we see language, too, as *flowing, fluent* and *outpouring*. For example, if I am too quick and nervous and jump in before you have finished what you are trying to say, you may be annoyed at being *cut off in mid-flow*. See also other entries on **expressivism, emotivism, solarity,** etc.

Mediated and immediate religion. Some religion is mediated, in the sense that the believer cannot approach the god immediately or directly, but needs to go through a mediator. Islam is a relatively immediate faith, in that it has no machinery for dispensing divine forgiveness, no priests and no sacraments. Each believer approaches God directly in his daily prayers. Certainly, the very highest veneration is accorded to the Qu'ran and to the Prophet, but one does not pray 'through' them, whereas in Christianity the believer has a high consciousness of sin which leads her to seek a sinless divine mediator, namely Jesus Christ, *through* whom she prays to God.

Traditional Church-Christianity eventually developed a very large apparatus of mediation. It included not only Christ and the Holy Spirit, but also the angels, the Blessed Virgin Mary and all the saints, the Scriptures, the multi-tiered priesthood, the sacraments, icons and much more – so much that in all periods there have been impatient folk who long to see the entire apparatus of mediation swept away with the arrival at last on earth of the long-awaited pure immediacy, 'the Kingdom of God on earth'.

In my scheme of thought, the Church is the classic example of mediated religion, and it is only an interim formation. The classic proclamation of immediate religion is Jesus' preaching of the Kingdom of God in Galilee. At the time of the Protestant Reformation a number of sects and movements attempted the changeover to immediate religion. Of them all, the most notable survivor is the Society of Friends. My own 'theology' is in a sense '*Quakerism-squared*', in that the great goal of attaining pure religious immediacy is only *fully* attained when the polar opposition between the human self and God has been overcome, by the full internalization of God within the self. The self and God become *concentric*. See **Kingdom-religion, theology**, above.

Metaphysical evil. In his *Theodicée* (1710), Leibniz distinguishes three main kinds of **evil**, *Moral*, *Physical* and *Metaphysical*.

Moral evil includes everything in **the human lifeworld** that is not as it should be, because of human sin. The traditional doctrines of the Fall and of Redemption claimed to show how God had provided a remedy for all evil of this kind, but at the very height of the Ages of Faith urban life was often hideously violent, and we can claim that better political arrangements, a more humane penal system, and a wide range of 'helping professions' and voluntary agencies have since done much to ameliorate the condition of the poor. It is reasonable to hope that more, much more, can yet be done.

Physical evil includes all the suffering brought about by disease, natural disasters etc. Much of this is the consequence of the way biological life has developed. In most species there is a huge overproduction of young. This gives the species a chance to recover its numbers very quickly after it has been depleted by a bad winter, but it is painful to see how tough life is for most of the young. On the other hand, modern medicine has in quite a short time been hugely successful the world over, giving rise to the hope that we may yet one day manage the world well.

Metaphysical evil includes what's left and cannot be over-come, namely, our finitude, our vulnerability to chance and our mortality. As our active life ends and we begin to decline, we know that we are on rails heading for our own extinction, and that there is nothing we can do about it.

From about 2000 I was aware that the 'metaphysical' kind of evil is the main religious problem now. The two other kinds of evil we can do something about, but the third remains to be coped with. There are some who claim that in time genetic engineering may conquer death, but I'm dubious about that. So far, our average span of life has been greatly extended by modern science, but we have not had much success in pro-longing our active life and even less in prolonging the peak period of our powers. Who wants to live through a hundred years and more of slow and steady decline, during which one long outlives everything one has done and been, until only a hoarse-voiced ghost of oneself remains? See also **solar living,** and note also the phrase **solar dying.**

Misandry, misotheism. Misandry, 'hatred of men, the male sex' is a modern coinage following the pattern of 'misogyny', hatred of women. I used the word in 1971, in connection with *The SCUM Manifesto* of Valerie Solanas, the woman who shot Andy Warhol. I claimed to be coining it, but some dictionaries now state that it goes back to the USA in the 1940s.

Misotheism, 'hatred of God' is another word only recently coined, as people have felt the need to draw a sharp distinction between *atheists*, people who live without God and say there is no God, and *misotheists* who actively hate God for being cruel, for letting them down, for turning out to be smugly indifferent to human suffering. Many militant atheists might be better described as misotheists, unless you think that what they really hate most is not God for not-existing, but the way so many people are damaged by ugly religious education.

'Your mind is in front of your face'. I use this slogan to attack the idea that the real you sits in a little spirit-chamber inside your head, perhaps looking at your retinas from behind them. No: it's *on the body-surface* that we produce and give off signs – words, body-language and so on – and it's on the body-surface that we pick up the signs given off by others. So the place of exchange is out on our surfaces and not in an interior space inside us.

When I was a child I had an encyclopedia which had a picture of the brain as a telephone exchange. Wires came into it from the external sense organs, and wires ran out of it to the muscles, etc. And, inevitably, there was a small person operating the exchange. I'm saying I want to cut out that small person. That is why I say that the visual field, together with its overlaps with hearing, touch etc., is in effect the field of consciousness and the place of exchange.

My theory interestingly confirms the ancient meaning and use of the word 'person'. A *persona* was a role in a play and by extension the mask you might put on in order to become the character you were playing. Hence 'impersonate'.

Mind, 'minding'. Do you *mind*? 'Minding' is the little space of heeding, hesitation, reflection and anxiety which comes to us with language and leads us to draw back a little from immediate and heedless engagement with life. The conscious being, having language, is reminded of other occasions like this one, similar events, precedents, parallels. So it can happen that we start to worry, to mind too much. '*Make your mind up*, won't you! Get on with it.'

This fascinating vocabulary of worrying and minding is one of the main sources of our ideas about what the human mind is. But I don't let it lead me back to belief in inner space. I simply retort that the worrier's 'Er, er', his dithering, his hesitation is also highly visible on his surface. There is no need at all to locate it inside his head.

Watch a two-year-old, trying to muster up the courage to set off down a long slide or chute, or perhaps the courage to jump into cold water. She is *visibly* 'in two minds'.

You may wonder why a religious person like me is so concerned about seemingly abstract questions in general philosophy. It is because I so much want to be a reasonably unified person, living one life in one world. I want to get rid of all forms of the distinction between matter and spirit, body and mind, this world and the next.

Our M/Other, or mother/other. If we are always in language, and if our thinking is in words and other signs, then we cannot hope to transcend language altogether and think beyond language. When we try to think the Ineffable, we can encounter only darkness. **The fountain** springs up for ever, but we cannot see where it's coming from. Even modern physics cannot go back further than 'quantum fluctuations in the vacuum', or Void.

I call this darkness our M/Other, but have also used the term O/Void, which puns upon Nothingness and a primal Egg and the term E/Vent, which puns upon 'Event' and 'vent'. In art we may find it symbolized by water pouring out ceaselessly from a jug. Imagine that, and then take away the jug, so that the water pours out for ever from no-thing.

I like to meditate on this darkness, and I think that it is more widespread in art than is usually recognized; but I would be reluctant to deify it.

Mysticism: '**Mysticism is not a kind of experience; it is a kind of transgressive writing**'. Apologists for religious experience often model their religious thought upon the appeal to sense-experience in early-modern science. As through sense-experience we can gradually build up a body of tested knowledge about the visible world, so through the spiritual experiences that some of us are fortunate enough to enjoy we can build up a body of knowledge about the spiritual world. Admittedly, many people are completely blind to religious feeling and experience, but the fact that some people happen to be blind to religion no more proves that religion is a waste of time than the fact that some people are deaf to music proves that music is a waste of time.

Arguments of this type have long been popular. But psychologists in particular will argue that religious experiences are everywhere shaped by the local religious beliefs, and philosophers will object to the idea that you can sensibly take our experience of seeing light or feeling warm as proving the truth of some transcendent belief. Where's the controlled experimental test of that sort of claim?

I have also tried to offer a different view of what religious experience in general and mysticism in particular are all about. Mystics are people who are very dissatisfied with **mediated religion**. They seek religious happiness through a kind of writing that tries to undermine or melt away the orthodox gulf between the soul and God. And at least they show that standard theology leaves many of the best people feeling highly dissatisfied.

In general, the people who have visions of the Blessed Virgin Mary are young Catholic girls approaching puberty, and she appears to them looking just like the statues of Mary in the church they attend. That's how they recognize her! Protestants and Buddhists don't see Mary. Interestingly, a Muslim girl's vision of Mary was reported from Egypt some years ago; but Mary figures in the Qu'ran, and Egypt is a country where Mary is a familiar figure because Muslims and Coptic Christians have lived there side-by-side for 13 centuries. Visions don't give information, but they do *express* our feelings.

N

Nihilism, from Latin *nihil*, nothing, is a term coined by Ivan Turgenev in his novel *Fathers and Sons* (1861). It expresses the reaction of a horrified older generation at the rise of young people who 'believed in nothing': they wanted to destroy existing institutions and in many ways anticipated the terrorists and suicide bombers of more recent years. *Philosophical* 'nihilism', invented by Nietzsche, was somewhat different. It was rather the full realization that from 'now on we are on our own': we no longer have anything external to ourselves to which we can look for salvation, or even guidance. Nietzsche often puts it plainly by saying: 'there is no moral world-order' – nothing guarantees that there will be a Happy Ending for good folk like ourselves.

On this view, nihilism is the doctrine that all **Grand Narratives** that purport to reassure us about our long-term future have now failed: this includes not only belief in the government of the world by a moral providence, but also Marxist narratives about historical materialism and liberal belief in progress by the growth of knowledge and enlightenment. In effect, the old creeds have broken down.

However, this is scarcely more than many or most Europeans now take for granted. I have put my own nihilism in the slogan: **'We are in the Void and we make the lot.'** We cannot rely upon anything quite external to ourselves. All we have to go on is the spontaneously uprushing **Fountain** of Life which wells up within us and takes on symbolic form as it passes out into **expression,** forming and colouring up **the human lifeworld.** In this my background inspiration seems to come particularly from painting after Impressionism – Post-Impressionism and Expressionism.

Notice also the similarity between modern nihilism and ancient eschatological beliefs, such as flourished in New Testament times. Amongst the most intense religious extremists belief that 'the end of all things is at hand' seems to imply that we can no longer trust in any received religious institutions, but must flee like refugees from external, **mediated religion** and make a fresh start on the basis of whatever resources we may find within ourselves.

Non-realism is a term widely used for the philosophy of God that I first set out in *Taking Leave of God* (1980). In that book I did indeed say that we need to break with our traditional theological **realism** (the view that theological statements purport to stand for objective theological facts about God etc., facts which do not depend on our faith in him. The realist holds that faith – especially in the great monotheistic traditions – is objectively oriented and makes objective claims.). Influenced by Kant's doctrine of God, I set out an alternative view of **God** as a guiding spiritual ideal and a necessary myth to live by. Trying to establish **the autonomy of religion,** I made God internal to religion, thus rejecting the old view which saw human religiousness as dependent upon, and as hoping to be vindicated by, an objectively existing God. In *The World to Come* (1982) I went a step further and defended 'theological pragmatism', a view which sees religious beliefs as 'regulative' or life-guiding. For example, it maintains that to speak of God as one's Father is not to describe God as being anything like one's biological parent, but to say that we should live confidently and be diligent, *as if* a fatherly eye watched over us. On this view, then, religious belief is very highly *practical*: it doesn't tell us facts about the Cosmos: it just shows us how we should live.

This did not satisfy my critics. My next line of defence was to say that I had never declared for straight atheism. My view was 'objectively atheous': I failed to affirm the objective God, but I wasn't proposing to do without God altogether. On the contrary, I still officiated in worship and prayed to God. So I called my intermediate position 'non-realism'. I did not hold a realist view of God, but nor did I reject God. On the contrary, I still *believed in* God; and belief-*in* is different from belief-*that*. Belief-in is a form of moral commitment to a person or a cause. I had lots of left-wing friends who in those far off days *believed in* socialism, but did not see themselves as obliged to claim that socialism, the real thing, actually existed in Cuba or Yugoslavia or somewhere like that. So it cannot just be assumed that *belief-in* something or other commits the believer to belief *that* it actually exists somewhere.

Nowadays I still think that my 'non-realist view of God' at that time was just about compatible with the historic orthodoxy. But time and events have moved on, and today I do not use the term 'non-realism', though it does still represent what many theologians privately think. And I am still very ready to point out that when believers recite the Creed, they are not thereby expressly committing themselves to a second para-Creed that defines how the first Creed is to be interpreted. No particular philosophy of religion has ever quite been declared *de fide* by the Western Church.

See also **Realism, Non-realism, Anti-realism.** Note that the psychologist C. G. Jung was a non-realist about the objective God but was also insistent upon the importance of the role of God in the life of the psyche. Thus at the end of his life he said emphatically in a television interview that he 'knew' God. In *The Sea of Faith* (1984) I was happy to invoke Jung as an ally – but I would not do so now. It is not 'solar' and it is not healthy to become so introspective that you begin to think that your inner, psychological world is more real than the common, public world. I'd put it more strongly than that: I don't believe in 'the inner life'. See also **Mind, 'minding'**.

O

Our world and The world. Since 1985 or so I have regularly distinguished our world from the world, saying that we know only the former and never the latter. Briefly, we see the world only from our human point of view and with our human senses. In addition, our knowledge is always 'discursive' – that is mediated by 'discourse' or language – and theory-laden. For example, when we look up at the night sky, do we see a black velvet cloth with holes in it through which twinkles the light of heaven? Or do we see living beings singing as they slowly rotate around us? Or do we see little suns at immense distances? At any rate, just considering those alternatives shows us how far we are from the absolute, intuitive and perspectiveless knowledge of the world that God was thought to possess and we hoped one day to share.

Can natural science hope one day to give us a knowledge of the world that is comparable with God's absolute knowledge? After Galileo and Descartes in the early seventeenth century, the 'world' as they called it, meaning in effect the solar system, came to be modelled as an elegant and precise machine that could be completely described in terms of matter, motion and number. For the present state of the world, using the model, we can predict any future state and then check with our own eyes to see if the prediction is fulfilled. If the model works and goes on working, we are justified in sticking with it.

But we have not got absolute knowledge, for all sorts of reasons. For example, we've proved only that predictions

83

(such as of eclipses) made with the help of the model have succeeded, so far. We have found that, so far, the model works – and that's all. But clever astronomers were already making successful astronomical predictions in antiquity, without anything like either Descartes's model or Newton's, and today we have in any case moved beyond Newton's physics and physicists have more than one model available to them. So it looks as if the original idea of Descartes, that his mathematical physics could give us knowledge of Nature just about as good as God's own knowledge of it, was clearly wrong.

He himself saw the difficulty. He needed to prove that there is a real world out there, on the far side of our sense-experiences, to which the cosmological model corresponds. He had to show that we are not systematically deceived like the humans in the film *The Matrix* (1999). He replied that he could prove the existence of God, who is a benevolent Creator and would not allow us to be deceived in our belief that there is a real world about us.

Thus Descartes, the chief founder of modern **philosophy**, tried to claim a bit too much for his mathematical physics and had to invoke God to guarantee his **realism** about human knowledge. After Descartes, the question before long became: But can we justify the objectivity of our knowledge *without* having recourse to God as its Guarantor? Can modern science go it alone? The best attempts to find a secular, only-human justification of our knowledge were made by Hume and above all, Kant. But nobody has *completely* succeeded to this day and the twentieth-century turn to language, *plus* extremely rapid change in physics, has only made the job harder.

Hence my saying about *our world* (the world as we know it, in our language and in our scientific theory) and *the world* (the world in itself, the world as it would appear to an omniscient, perspectiveless observer). *Our World* is the everyday human world, hugely extended by our scientific theory. It is the world given us by our language, ordinary with a big specialist supplement. *The World*, a purely objective world known by a Knower who transcends language, space and time, is an idea we've got to give up. All our knowledge is mediated by language and theory. It's only human, fallible and provisional.

Many religious believers have been brought up to think of their own faith as accessing unchanging dogmatic **Truth**. Real, capital-T, Truth. It is hard for them to recognize that the only-human, fallible and provisional kind of knowledge that science has given us is far and away the best way to knowledge that human beings have ever discovered.

Outsidelessness. I keep using this term by way of trying to show that all dreams of being able to jump quite clear of our selves, our world, our language, our human condition, are vain. I'm arguing for thoroughgoing immanence. There is only one world – the everyday **human lifeworld**.

Here are one or two simple examples of outsidelessness. The surface of a sphere is outsideless, in that you never come to its edge, or its corners. Talk of 'going to the ends of the Earth', or of its 'four corners', is misguided. Again, the Universe in modern physics is finite but unbounded. It has no fence around its edges: you never come to the end of it. Interestingly, space-time *itself* has no outside. Wittgenstein was a strong teacher of outsidelessness, for example in the simple phrase: *Our life is endless, as the visual field is endless*. Life has no outside.

I argue that it is better to give up traditional dreams of transcendence and have described the jump back into immanence as **entostasy** – the opposite of ecstasy. We ordinarily think that the way to eternal happiness is by *ascesis*, or climbing a long ladder or stairway to heaven. But I have argued for the *superior* religious happiness – and even, the superior unification of the human self – that is to be had by returning fully into immanence and there practising **solar living**. See also **God is a secular humanist**.

85

P

'Be passers-by': an interesting, isolated saying of Jesus from the Gospel of Thomas (42), attractive to me because passing by, in Latin, is transiting: 'be transients', it instructs us, reminding us that through most of human history human beings were nomads who flitted over the landscape, leaving little permanent mark upon it. In the world of classical antiquity communications of every kind were slow and very expensive. Teachers of any new message in religion or **philosophy** were commonly obliged to become wandering evangelists who carried a cloak, a wallet and one book. Spreading the word required the dedication of one's life to perpetual vagrancy. Later, as the institutional Church became relatively wealthy and settled, it switched values and began to pronounce very strongly in favour of the settled kind of life. Too much unofficial travelling, whether by bishops or by monks, was now censured. Instead the new ideal was that, at least as soon as you were adult and (if lay) married, you should spend all your life in one place – both literally and metaphorically.

The ideal of stability remained strong until the Industrial Revolution, which has made us progressively more mobile. By today, many or most of us would probably say that we like the intellectual stimulus of life in a highly mobile, multi-ethnic and multi-faith world. We are all much less rigid in our beliefs and attitudes than were the old-style country folk who knew only one world and only one way of doing everything. We now don't feel so threatened by strangers or by change; indeed, we actually *enjoy* social and cultural difference.

In this context, one can see why Church Christianity was closely matched to agricultural civilization: a fixed set of beliefs, a stable, relatively unchanging way of life and an annual liturgical calendar closely matched to the annual cycle of seasonal agricultural tasks. By contrast, 'Kingdom' religion is more appropriate to our modern globalized and mobilized world of torrentially rapid communication and social change.

In the old order everything was laid on for you readymade. You just accepted it all and stayed put. In the new order, where nothing is fixed and everything has to come out of us, we are wanderers again and in danger of being over-nostalgic for a lost Eden, a rural idyll. But the rule is that – as Everyman finds in the old play – as we go on and get older 'knowledge' (that is the comfort of living within a fixed system of certainties) progressively fades away, until the only support left to us is 'love' (that is the ethical) and we walk the very last steps of the journey stark naked into the grave. So be happy to be a beliefless 'passer-by'. You're going the way of all flesh.

A friend points out that the term **passers-by** cannot help but recall Luke's parable of the Good Samaritan, whose hero is precisely the one who does *not* 'pass by' but stops and attends to the needs of a complete stranger. A fair point, and one well illustrated by medical ethics, which requires a doctor who is a paying customer in a theatre or on an aircraft to step forward at once, declare him- or herself and attend a fellow customer who has been taken ill. But note that both in **Buddhism** and in Christianity there are many stories of monks or friars who, just because they were itinerants, travelling people, were ethically very quick to respond to a moral need when they met it. Travelling light, and reducing the quantity of one's possessions and one's regular commitments, ought to be morally liberating.

Everything is a Period Piece. In some ways, the newer visual media are making everyone a historicist. We marvel at the way someone with expert knowledge can immediately tell where and when almost any object was produced. That is, the expert sees at once to which historical totality it *must* belong. It's easy. Everything is unmistakeably a period piece. So well do ordinary people now grasp this that they are quick to spot and to ridicule anachronisms in any kind of costume drama. If a script-writer makes a careless mistake it's obvious to many or most viewers that at that particular period they simply didn't say that sort of thing. They just didn't think like that. That's not how it was.

'Everything is a period piece' means briefly that everything is a product of some particular cultural totality and is quite unmistakeably so. So well do people now understand this that every decade of the past 120 years now has a very distinctive flavour of its own, a flavour common to all products of that period, *including its ideas about religion and morality.*

People like to think that some meanings and some values persist unchanged through time. Some US citizens may suppose that their written Constitution of 1776 is timelessly valid, like scripture; but historians and lawyers know very well that the context, social and cultural, within which the Constitution document was originally written and signed was very different indeed from the modern United States of America. To keep its place in American life, the Constitution has had to be continuously rethought, reimagined, reinterpreted, almost re-invented, from then until now.

Many theologians will now say the same about the Bible and even about Christianity itself. To stay apparently the same, you have to reinvent yourself continuously. That's true even of seemingly 'unchanging' institutions like the Vatican and the Papacy. Just think, for example, of how different from each other the Popes have been since Pius XII and of how they have struggled to maintain an appearance of constancy in tumultuous times. And the same is true even of 'fundamentalists', as any historian can quickly show. Indeed, so rapid is the pace of change now that everyone of us who has lived through three or more decades since puberty now recognizes that *we ourselves* too change with the times. Each of us is a somewhat different person in each decade.

Against this background I have long argued that the greatest threat to traditional Church-Christianity now comes, not from the natural sciences, but from *history*; and in particular from our historicist realization that *everything* is part of a slowly evolving totality that lives by re-inventing itself. So my 'constructivism' – the doctrine that we collectively are continuously making, unmaking and remaking our world and all our 'truths' is no more than what every ordinary person now knows very well. With **the Death of God** the old ready-made and stable Cosmos died, too. So did all ideas of an extra-historical 'core self' or 'immortal soul' in us. My supposedly crazy or satanic religious ideas are no more than platitudes that everyone in his or her heart already accepts.

Philosophy. When at the beginning of the twentieth century Ernest Rhys edited the largest and best-known series of re-prints of great books, Everyman's Library (London: Dent and Dutton), he included works by fifteen or so of the great philosophers from the Western canon, starting with three volumes of Plato and ending (eventually) with Nietzsche's *Zarathustra* (no. 892).

It could not happen today – though it must be conceded that the Penguin Classics series has over the years done very well by some philosophers, notably Plato and Nietzsche. Otherwise, and for various reasons, British philosophy has tended to be Eurosceptic and has not paid much attention to the history of philosophy. The people who write, publish and review 'trade' books have mostly read English or other literary subjects at university and philosophy is somehow not 'literature'. In any case, the British have been heavily influenced by the traditional Protestant view that the Bible is sufficient in religion and by their own traditional love of experience and experiment – that is, natural science. Nowadays, the sciences reckon to be taking over much of the traditional subject-matter of philosophy – for example, the 'mind', consciousness, language, space and time – and it is by and large to the scientists and *not* to philosophers that society nowadays looks for pronouncements upon the great mysteries of existence.

Nevertheless and in spite of the unfriendly climate, I have to persist in my view that the only way out of the present crisis in religious thought is by philosophy. We have to go back to the kind of thinking that prevailed at the beginning of the Western tradition, a kind of thinking in which philosophy and religious thought had not yet become distinguished from each other.

89

'Poetical' theology and philosophy. Plato is such a universal thinker that his writings already include many of the best arguments against his own views. He is the chief source of the Western notion that beyond the world of everyday life and sense-experience there has to be a higher, invisible, 'spiritual' world, an Order of Reason, an intelligible world of Ideas. It's philosophy's equivalent of the Heaven of religion. But in the *Republic* Socrates points out that our language is completely embedded in and attuned to the requirements of our life in this world. How can it possibly be used to describe another, entirely different world?

The question is devastating and was eventually to prove fatal to all ideas that we can somehow climb clear of our ordinary human circumstances and limitations and ascend above ourselves to enter a quite different world, whilst yet somehow remaining truly ourselves. In the long run, **philosophy** was bound to break with metaphysics, with supernatural theology and with all ideas of **life after death**, instead concluding that there is only one world, and it is *this* world. *Our life has no outside.* Philosophy must end with naturalism – but we need to keep on going over and over the arguments in order to get a clear vision of the human situation as we now understand it.

In my own religious philosophy I do not attempt to reinstate *either* metaphysics *or* supernatural theology. Instead I tried to do a 'poetical' kind of theology and philosophy, which binds the world together, *not* by hooking us all on to something transcendent, but instead by using a strong poetic metaphor to unify our vision of our condition. The favourite metaphors are mostly old ones: Light, the Sun, **the Fountain**, **Fire** and **Life**. I try to deploy these metaphors in such a way as to generate a vision that helps to reconcile us to life and shows us how we should live in order to attain the best there is for us.

The word 'poetry' derives from a Greek word meaning 'making' (*poiēsis*). Nietzsche's idea of 'strong' poetry conveys what I am after. It suggests that a poetical theology might be seen as a consoling and inspiring work of art.

Postmodernism. A word that, after a brief vogue, is now somewhat *démodé*. I wrote a quartet of books that were self-consciously postmodern in the late 1980s: *Life Lines*, *The Long Legged Fly*, *The New Christian Ethics* and *Radicals and the Future of the Church*. The chief philosophical progenitor of postmodernism was Nietzsche, who thought that the optimism and reforming zeal of the Enlightenment and of the Romantic Movement had grossly over-reached itself and had crashed. The 'spectre haunting Europe' was not socialism, as Karl Marx had said, but **nihilism**.

Perhaps things are not quite as bad as Nietzsche thought. At the height of the 1960s people experienced the collapse of all traditional authority as a liberation. They were for a while filled with utopian hope. Today, the utopianism has faded, and many of the old problems have returned. More than ever, we find ourselves trying to improvise remedies. Perhaps the legacy of the Sixties is simply that we have lost all the old **Grand Narratives**, all the old readymade **Answers** and all the old certainties. We are on our own, making it all up as we go along.

Primary and Secondary. Aristotle points out that in **philosophy** the order in which you treat your topics makes a big difference to the conclusions you will reach. Taking up the idea, Thomas Aquinas assumes that you should follow the 'order of being'. God, being the Creator, is always the First Cause of everything, while at the same time there is amongst his creatures in the world of Nature an order of 'secondary causes'. So there is a 'vertical', 'constitutive' relation to God the Universal Creator and at the same time a 'horizontal' network of natural or secondary causes. Thus a person could say *both* that 'God is my Maker' *and* that 'my parents brought me into being', without formal contradiction.

The idea gets extended in various ways. Thus an individual substance, a particular thing, is 'primary' and its attributes or qualities are 'secondary'. There is also talk of primary and secondary qualities: for example, when the qualities that are inherent in a thing are called 'primary', whereas qualities that arise from its effect upon our sense-organs (such as its taste or its colour) are called 'secondary'.

The primary/secondary distinction was very commonly used, especially in medieval philosophy, to conjure up a vision of the Universe as hierarchically ordered in every part. The right thing to do, in philosophy, in religion and in ethics, always involved due respect for everything's place in the order of things. There were animal, vegetable and mineral 'Kingdoms'. Human society was similarly ordered, apparently by God, and you should accept the place he has assigned you to.

It goes without saying that science has little time for such ideas, but even so great a figure as Darwin had to make little notes to remind himself to be wary of speaking about 'higher' and 'lower' animals. Even he could make the mistake of thinking of some races of humans as being 'higher' than others (in general, peoples who lived further North were 'higher', which was bad news for the inhabitants of Tierra del Fuego).

Developed medieval religious thought was very keen indeed on ideas of hierarchical order, and it is not surprising that so much of modern thought has been attempting to get rid of them. My desire to move from Church-Christianity (which is always very hierarchical) to **Kingdom-religion** (which is Quakerish and ultra-democratic) belongs in this context. When I talk about **the mysticism of secondariness** I mean that I am often enraptured by the visual beauty of things that stood near the very bottom of the old scales of being and value. The 'passing show of existence' – everything 'merely' sensuous and transient – should not be regarded as a deceitful temptation. On the contrary, we should regard our eyes and ears as organs of religious experience and should train them accordingly, instead of shutting both, as people used to do when at their prayers. See also **Mysticism**.

R

Realism, Non-realism, Anti-realism. It very often happens nowadays that a technical term invented by an academic or other specialist is taken into ordinary language – but in a slightly different sense. For example, the term *food-chain* was invented by zoologists to describe a series in which each item gets eaten by the next member, until we reach the predator at the top of the food-chain. The famous example is that of DDT, an agricultural insecticide which in the 1950s nearly wiped out Britain's birds of prey. As it went up the food-chain from plants to caterpillars, to birds and then to raptors, the insecticide became steadily more concentrated until it reached the hawks at the top of the food-chain. That illustrates the scientific use of the term; but when today people concerned about the safety of our food say that they don't want GM crops to 'enter the human food-chain', they are using the term in a quite different sense. They seem to mean just the human food system by which food passes from farms to tables.

The term *realism* is another example. In everyday use it may mean 'a concern for the facts and for what is practicable', or it may be used to mean something like 'truth to life and freedom from illusions and sentimentality' – what Italians call *verismo* in opera and cinema. But philosophers have a different use, derived from old, old controversies about the legacy of Plato. He left us with the idea that the world of our sense-experience is just a stream of transient particulars. The general ideas and abstract concepts with the help of which we can see the world as an ordered Cosmos are not *themselves* objects of perception, so Plato taught that they existed in a distinct world of Ideas to which our reason gives us access. Others would later argue that Plato's Ideas are just concepts in our heads (Aristotle's view), or indeed that they are just words (medieval nominalism and much modern philosophy); but Plato himself believed in a *real* world of Ideas.

Let us now turn to some modern forms of realism. A *platonist* or *realist* in the philosophy of mathematics holds that the truth of true expressions in mathematics is not dependent upon our minds, but is *objective*, whereas a conventionalist will say that maths is a lot of useful games and skills invented by us. Truth in maths is therefore like truth in chess: it is truth within a system that we ourselves have made up.

What about morality? Certainly great numbers of ordinary people are convinced that many of our most widely agreed general rules in morality are somehow objectively true. They are realists; but it is notoriously hard to say convincingly what moral realism claims. Do values and virtues – or at least, some of them – exist objectively; and if so, then how and where? It is very hard to find a convincing answer, and it is not surprising, in view of the huge moral changes that have occurred within the past sixty years or so, that many ethical non-realists will want to argue that morality as a whole is human, socially evolved and that it slowly changes over the centuries.

Now to the question of **God**. A theistic realist is a person who believes (along with Pope Pius X's *motu proprio* 'Sacrorum Antistitum', 1910), that the existence of God can be proved by unassisted human reason. God would still exist out there even if there were no human being alive who actually believed in him. The 'God of the philosophers' really exists, independent of our faith in him, and a Latin Christian who takes this view may very well be ready to accept that Jews and Muslims worship basically the same God, though holding different views about which of them possess in their scriptures God's latest and final **Revelation** of his will for us.

The non-realist about God, taking his cue from Kant, will usually argue at least that the traditional proofs of God's existence have now broken down, but the idea of God continues to function as a guiding and inspiring ideal of reason. He will then often argue that each developed religious tradition is like a language-game. In a theistic religion such as Christianity, look at the way talk of God works within the Christian system. Similarly what Muslims mean by God (Allah) is fully spelt out *within their religious system*. So on this account we need not spend time on the question of God's *objective* existence. It is enough to show how each religious system works and how it is that God is 'real' for faith. Now the thought may strike us: *Why do we suppose it necessary to demand any extra-religious reality of God?* God is real, within the system and for the believer. The non-realist therefore is a person who simply refrains from urging God's objective existence and prefers to show that God truly has a sort-of reality for the believer, within the system. On this basis, different religious systems can co-exist peaceably within the same society.

An anti-realist takes a somewhat stronger view. The term was invented by Nietzsche, who insisted that the time had come to break with the legacy of Plato and to invent a new way of thinking.

Amongst recent philosophers of religion, the late D. Z. Phillips is a good example of a Wittgensteinian non-realist. John Hick, often in dispute with Phillips, is still (just about) a traditional realist about God. At least, Hick still maintains that we should do the best we can to deliver a realistic account of God and of **life after death,** so as to give comfort to afflicted people. For my part, I began as a (broadly orthodox) realist who emphasized the Negative Way and the practical bearing of religious belief. But in *Taking Leave of God* (1980), I declared for non-realism and then by the late 1980s was a clear anti-realist – probably influenced by Nietzsche's view that Kantian non-realism was a weak position that could not be held for long. I still maintained an Impossible Love for God until around 2007. See also **The Autonomy of Religion, Buddhism, Impossible Loves** and **Non-realism.**

Does Religion need an Object? Judaism, Christianity and Islam are all strongly *theocentric*, in the sense that God is the central concern of every believer's life. One should seek above all to do God's will, to seek God's forgiveness and Grace, to worship God, to draw near to God and in the end 'to know

God and enjoy him for ever'. English law, and the standard English dictionaries, still understand religion and define it in theocentric terms.

However, the West has always been aware of the Epicurean vision of the good life, which is *not* theocentric. The gods do exist, but they are far away and unconcerned with us. There is no reason why we should trouble ourselves with trying to approach them. It is possible to be content with mild scepticism, freedom from anxiety, serenity and a gentle, moderate enjoyment of the good things in life. The Epicurean is an objective theist, but is not theocentric in his religion. He thinks there are gods, but he doesn't *believe in* them.

Going further, the Jains and the Buddhists very commonly – at least, in Asia – also acknowledge that there are or may well be gods and lesser spirits, and both of them are undoubtedly highly developed religious systems. But the kind of calm, emptied-out blessedness that Jains and Buddhists seek is certainly *not* theocentric. They follow an ascetical Path to a blessed state of the soul which is empty and objectless. Evidently there can be and are objectless religious systems.

Can Christianity be interpreted as, or become, similarly objectless? There are at least some suggestions that it can. In the final world that is looked out for by both the Hebrew prophets and the early Christians God pours out his own Spirit into our hearts, God comes to dwell amongst us, and God even becomes himself human and suffers the common human fate. Thus in the classic Judaeo-Christian scheme of thought, God is out there and over against us *only* during the period in which we humans are alienated from God, namely the period between the Fall and the final Kingdom. In the perfect state of the world, religion is immediate, and God is internalized – that is, non-objective. See also **Realism, etc., Kingdom-religion.**

Religious Experience. One effect of the Romantic Movement upon religious thought was to shift the emphasis away from the question 'Exactly what religious beliefs do you hold?' and towards the question: 'What does it *feel* like to be a believer?' During the early nineteenth century the first scholarly studies of religious experience and of mysticism were published and in due course people began to ask 'How can we tell whether a religious experience is veridical, or genuine?' and 'Can we use religious experience as evidence for the truth of religious beliefs?'

This question had been raised in the past, but philosophers had usually been dismissive. Thomas Hobbes, in the mid seventeenth century, put it shortly: 'If a man tells me that God spoke to him in a dream, all I know is that he dreamt that God spoke to him.' Joseph Butler in the mid eighteenth century sees religion in terms of morality and one's conscience and describes the Methodist appeal to vivid religious experiences as 'a very horrid thing'. Towards the end of the same century, Kant thinks that whereas conscience and morality are universal (that is, we can reasonably expect every normal human being to acknowledge their authority), mystical experience is too odd and too rare for a philosopher to know what to make of it.

The Romantic Movement gradually changed all this. Many medieval and baroque mystical and devotional writers were reprinted, and eventually one major book appeared: *The Varieties of Religious Experience* (1902) by the philosopher-psychologist William James (1842–1910). During the half-century after James, a number of Roman Catholic writers explored the possibility of a new apologetics based upon a careful description and analysis of Catholic experience.

Since the 1960s, however, this line of argument has been decisively refuted by the counter-attack which says all religious experiences are already shaped by the beliefs of the experient, and therefore there are no 'pure' and 'innocent' religious experiences. If a religious experience really were a pure datum, how could we *recognize* it? Our religious experiences, if we are so fortunate as to have them, *express* our faith and cannot be called upon to prove it. See also **Mysticism, Fact and Interpretation.**

Ressentiment. A French word for feeling, taken up and used by Nietzsche to describe the wide range of negative or 're-active' feelings, often suppressed, that may be aroused in us when we encounter other people. These reactive emotions include suspicion, envy, jealousy, hatred, anger and simple wariness. Among the active or positive feelings, Spinoza mentions sanity (which I suppose is just mental good health), joy, love and the sense of freedom. These are strongly affirmative and outgoing feelings, without any inhibition, whereas the reactive emotions (which Spinoza calls 'passive') tend to be at least partly suppressed and to 'poison the soul'.

I accept, of course, this **emotivist** and **expressivist** model of the life of a human self. The next step is to say that the greatest ethical teachers – the Buddha, Jesus, Nietzsche – all wanted to live completely without ressentiment. But in their teaching about how we can achieve such a state, they differ significantly. The Buddha seeks through meditation and a very moderate style of life to achieve freedom from the violence of the passions. Nietzsche's ideal is 'noble': one should affirm **life** and do one's own thing as 'a free spirit' who does not even *notice* the wrongs done to him by others. Jesus' way is almost what I've heard called *ecstatic naturalism*: one should love life so intensely that one's love spills over everything, including even one's enemies. **Solarity** precludes even the slightest ressentiment.

In brief, the Buddha teaches coolness, Nietzsche teaches magnanimity, greatness of soul, and Jesus teaches completely generous love.

Revelation is Latin for 'unveiling'. The equivalent Greek word is *apocalypse*, 'uncovering' or perhaps 'exposing'. The background idea is of a prophet or seer in trance, through whose mouth God gives us advance warning of great things that will shortly be happening. Such a revelation from God may be sought urgently in a period when God's people are having a very bad time and are desperate for reassurance that their deliverance will come soon.

In scriptural religions, the word revelation particularly refers to a body of 'saving truths' about God and about what he has done for our salvation. The saving truths are extracted from scripture, which may be described as *being the Word of God*, or as *containing the Word of God*. More cautiously still, some twentieth-century theologians spoke of the Bible as *bearing witness to the saving acts of God in history*. In which case the revelation is given primarily in the (allegedly) historical events. The Bible witnesses to those events and supplies us with an authoritative theological interpretation of them. This theory has the advantage of taking the site of revelation out of the Bible and into the history of 'the Word of God incarnate'.

However, this does not entirely resolve our difficulties. The historical status of the Old Testament is currently in flux, so I set it aside here. In the case of the New Testament, how can one *recognize* some event as an 'act of God in history', unless one *already has* the concepts of God and of an act of God in history? In any case, there seems to be little doubt that with careful attention to all the sources, a persuasive secular critical-historical account of Christian origins can be given. Few reputable New Testament scholars, surely, now claim that the available evidence can be accounted for only by invoking supernatural causes.

My own view, then, is that we should learn to do without the notion of revelation. Nothing's hidden: there is no secret. The very notion of God as one who 'speaks to us' – presumably in one or more of our natural human languages – is not 'realistically' believable. In general, where supernaturally caused events or divine revelations are in question we do not have, and perhaps can scarcely imagine having, good criteria for distinguishing between the real thing and the various sorts of error, fraud and delusion. In a case like that of the Oracle at Delphi, does any historian today suggest that perhaps the Oracle was genuine and that a god really *did* speak out of that cave? Of course not.

S

The Secularization Thesis. Historically, secularization was the transfer of authority over a certain area of life from the Church to the 'temporal power', the State. Education and the making and administration of the law about marriage and divorce are examples of the process.

Against this background, many people have believed for perhaps two or three centuries that a large-scale and long-term process of secularization is gradually transforming the whole of our culture, as the religious realm or sphere of life slowly contracts until eventually the majority of the population can and do live almost their entire lives without giving religion a thought. It survives within the private sphere as a kind of ancestral loyalty, but it no longer has any public influence.

The process takes surprisingly different forms in different countries. In the USA, Church and State have always officially been separate, but religion remains strong and no leading politician can be publicly non-religious, whereas in England the Church is still established although it has shrunk alarmingly in the past 150 years. In France, once 'the eldest daughter' of the Catholic Church, secularization has proceeded gradually since the Revolution of 1789 and is now far advanced. Ireland, Spain and Poland, all of them once very Roman Catholic, have all for different reasons seen rather rapid secularization during the past 30 years.

Something similar has happened in many other culture-areas outside the West. In the heyday of colonialism many people in the Middle East and in India, for example, were led to think of their own religion as backward and decadent. But the interest of Western scholars in their cultural traditions has inspired attempts to revive Islam and Hinduism.

So it is that in many parts of the world today, the cultural dominance of the West and a steady process of secularization and globalization still continue, but are sharply opposed by neo-conservative 'fundamentalists' in several faiths and in most countries. The neo-conservatives sharply deny that any process of long-term secularization is 'inevitable'. On the contrary, they say, 'God is back'; a rediscovery of our religious heritage will lead us back to faith.

Most radical Christian theologians – and I among them – take a different and intermediate view. We say that the secularization thesis is true and that the old pre-scientific religious cultures and world-views are everywhere in headlong decline. But this great cultural change should not be seen as the complete elimination of religion. On the contrary, modern, globalized people are still acutely aware of a personal need for spirituality, of the transience of **life** and of the finality of **death**. People still have religious needs. Furthermore, Christian radicals regard secularization as a fulfilment of Christianity. In the old theology, God in Christ has secularized *himself*, being content to enter history, become human and die. Globalization is the realization of the Pentecostal hope that one day all nations will be united, rather than divided, by religion. Besides, in the old Biblical myth the story of the human race, from Eden to the Kingdom of God, starts and finishes *on this Earth*. The Bible is not nearly as otherworldly in its orientation as Catholic Christianity eventually became.

So it is possible for a radical like me to welcome the 'end of the Middle Ages', the end of supernatural theology and the end of an era when you spent the whole of this life preparing for another life yet to come. Instead, we need to acknowledge that this world is already the last world. There is no further life beyond this one. So we should turn towards this world and concentrate on living life to the full while we have it. Spirituality and ethics will thus be seen in terms of loving life and seeking to add value to it, *now* and in the present moment. When we are no longer oriented towards eternity, we may come to accept that all being is temporal, everything just pours out and passes away and we with it.

Solar ethics, solar living, solar loving, solar expressivism, solarity. The idea of 'solar ethics' first appears in my *After*

All (1994, p. 109), where the Sun appears not as a symbol for life-giving cosmic monarchy, but as a symbol of pure affirmation. The Sun is **all out, actus purus**: it *is* its own continuous self-outpouring. It burns so fiercely that it is everliving, ever-dying, by one and the same process of pouring itself continuously out into **expression**.

This metaphor then led towards an ethic of active, emotional self-expression, in which I took up ideas from Spinoza's distinction between the active and passive emotions and from Nietzsche's ethic of life-affirmation.

The use of the sun as a metaphor for how we should live crops up here and there in literature. An Anthony Burgess novel is titled *Living Like the Sun*, and there is an aria in praise of solarity in Gilbert and Sullivan. An early Buddhist panel in the British Museum depicts the Buddha as an enthroned solar disc. In ordinary language a very animated, outgoing person is commonly described as *sparkling, glowing, shining* and *radiant*. **Etty Hillesum** is cited more than once in this book as an exceptional modern figure who discovered and practised solar living in the most extreme circumstances one could imagine.

Another way of approaching and explaining solar ethics is by way of describing it as living purely affirmatively and without any **ressentiment** at all. See also *Solar Ethics* (1995), **Introvertive and Extravertive religion and mysticism, Inside out** and entries under **Life**.

A Spirituality is a religious life-style. The word 'life-style' became popular during the early 1970s. It shows that people have become aware that the old 'spirituality', in which you withdrew from everything outward, turned into yourself and sought to cultivate an interior, hidden, secret life of the soul is dead. No: as people turn away from the old introverted Western spirituality and from 'organized' religion, they want to come out into the open and find a new 'extravertive' or 'outgoing' style of living *in public*. It is well known that gay people, male and female, have developed this vocabulary of **'coming out'** particularly well and indeed have almost made a religion of it. They are quite right: a properly developed postmodern spirituality will be an outgoing, affirmative life-style. We want to be able to express ourselves fully, *be ourselves* and do our thing, in *public*. The old split psychology, which had us living an outer life as ordinary citizens of this world, while simultaneously living an inner life in dialogue with God and the heavenly world, is now intolerable. The attempt to live two lives in one world is absurd: we should *live out* one life in one world. And in *living out* – that is, in pouring out into **expression** and passing away all the time – we find the highest religious happiness there can be for us.

T

Can you tell what it is? A line from the Vulgate Psalter declares that 'the Heavens are telling the Glory of God' – and the word for telling is 'they *narrate*'. The verb *tell* is interestingly ambiguous. It may be used to mean, 'Can you discern, or descry, or *make out* what it is?' where we are talking to someone who is screwing up her eyes as she tries to decide what it is that she is looking at. So the verb 'to tell', like the expression 'to *make out*' and other phrases to do with *construing, constructing* and *putting a construction upon*, brings out vividly that in perceiving things we don't just mirror the world. We build, we interpret, we put into words.

The belief that in perception the mind passively mirrors the external world is often associated with John Locke, who speaks of the mind before experience as being a *tabula rasa*, a blank slate. Modern experimental psychology and modern philosophy are leading us to a very different view. We are world-builders. Note here the closeness of *my life* to *my world*, which is revealed when someone emerging from a sharp rupture in life says: 'I've got to build a new life for myself'. See also **Make Out**, etc.; **Fact and Interpretation**.

A theatrical view of the self. For centuries European writers have compared human society with a theatre *stage*, or with a *market*. On the market-model, we are constantly in the business of *exchange*, as we negotiate or bargain with each other, trying to get the best deal we can. On the theatrical model, we put much time and energy into display – as for example when people parade in the evenings along a recognized route such as Las Ramblas in Barcelona, or sit on one of the benches near it to 'watch the world go by'. In the past young people of both sexes spent much of their available funds on buying a fine costume for the new season. Both sexes displayed and of course both sexes may play the game, and act out their roles with a flourish, in the various relationships of their life.

In my philosophy – and in particular, in **solar ethics** – I opt strongly for the theatrical model, which sees a person as a role. As we may admire an old trouper who can still dress up and do his thing, so in ethics being solar involves *putting on a good show*, *strutting one's stuff*, *being game* and *doing one's thing*. Why? – because *the show must go on*. Anyway, we cannot help but be touched by their courage when people turn out and *make the most of what they've got*.

Theology, 'Poetical theology'. Nearly all of what today passes for theology is in fact merely historical theology, which is safe. Doing theology head-on, in an autologous, creative and confessional style, is perilous. It invites scorn, it makes enemies. The position appears to be that we all know in our hearts that the old faith isn't actually true any more, but we'd all of us prefer to continue for as long as we possibly can in a state of ironical half-belief and slow decline. The fool who insists that the game is up and it's all over arouses embarrassment and hostility.

By way of trying to break out of this stagnation, I have suggested that we need to break with all traditional authorities and revealed truths and go back to a time when **philosophy** and theology were not yet clearly distinguished. We should experiment: we should try to make a fresh start, for example by writing a kind of poetical theology. We don't start from the data of **revelation**, and we don't try to do metaphysics. Instead, we try to write 'strong poetry', asking for example how far one of the classic religious images can link together various areas of our experience in a consoling way, and so help us to **say Yes to life.**

What images? Twenty years ago I was ruminating on **Being** and **Life** and then moved to consider dealing with them under the images of the Sun, or light generally, or **the Fire**, or **the Fountain**. Developing these images, might it be possible to devise a new kind of secular and purely 'poetical' religious thought, which would help us to cope with our own transience?

Therapeutic Religion and Philosophy. It has often been remarked that the Buddha's teaching is cast in a medical idiom: first he gives a detailed diagnosis of what is wrong with us, and then he prescribes the remedy. The Four Noble Truths explain the causes of our unhappiness, and the Eightfold Path shows us the way towards a state of cool well-being.

There is something similar in the Western tradition, too. Kant's *Critique of Pure Reason* includes, in the Dialectic, an account of certain errors and metaphysical illusions to which the human mind is peculiarly prone. When we learn from Kant what these illusions are we can gain freedom from them and will be ready to accept without complaint the human condition as it is and the limits of thought for what they are.

In particular, Kant proposes to cure us of the illusions of dogmatic metaphysics, which are (roughly) that by unassisted human reason we can gain metaphysical knowledge of what God, the soul and the world really are. Give up the illusions of metaphysics, and we can learn to be content with natural science, the Critical philosophy and a purely moral kind of faith.

Wittgenstein goes further than Kant. In his later thought, he is a sort of 'anti-philosopher', whose philosophy is a procedure for curing people of the various disabling intellectual worries and anxieties that threaten their happiness. Indeed, Wittgenstein's ideas in many respects foreshadow today's very popular 'Cognitive Behaviour Therapy' (CBT).

I cannot help but stand in this tradition. But my 'poetical' philosophy and theology hopes to engage the imagination and the feelings of the reader, so that we can the more easily learn to say Yes to life as it is.

The Torus is an image of the Cosmos, of 'It all', that figured in *After All* and *The Fountain*. It is best described as a fat doughnut, a doughnut so fat that its central hole is reduced to a point. That point is the beginning and the end of the world, the initial singularity from which the expanding universe arises and spreads as a widening circle on the surface of the Torus. Reaching the point of its maximum extension, it then returns on the underside of the Torus, back into its own beginning. As it returns it recoups all the energy expended in its expansion. And since the Torus is seen as if from the standpoint of eternity, where there is no 'before' or 'after', the whole cycle of expansion and return is seen as a self-existent Whole. This image of It all resembles many traditional images of God, while to those who live somewhere on the surface of the Torus all be-ing seems to be temporal and contingent.

Interestingly, Roger Penrose of Oxford has recently proposed a cyclical model of the cosmos. But to me it represents something of a temptation. It's too alluring.

This is It, That's It, Was that It?, What's It all about?, It all, Are you up for It? I love these very suggestive it-idioms, which were discussed in *The Meaning of It All in Everyday Speech*. We seem often to use the word It to signify the not-self, what we are up against in general, It All. At other times it is something big and perhaps life-changing that we await with excitement and a touch of dread. The very fact that the pronoun is neuter suggests that there is something fearsome about a being that is non-sexual and therefore non-human, and in cinema the word 'It' in a film-title usually signifies a monster or something of the kind. But this is too weak and timid a response. If we embrace It all, then we may find ourselves saying afterwards that we now love It all, everything about It.

It is a particularly vivid example of my contention that on analysis we can find a surprising amount of theology lurking within the simplest idioms in our everyday speech.

Totum simul (Latin: all at once). From ancient philosophy we have inherited a distinction between discursive and intuitive knowledge. *Discursive knowledge* is mediated by discourse, language, and so is spread out in time, so that we know things bit-by-bit, 'in a glass darkly' and fragmentarily. This is contrasted with an ideal condition that we hope perhaps to attain at the end of our life, or after it, when our knowledge will be *intuitive*, immediate, complete and visionary – an absolute, divine, blessedness-giving kind of knowledge, 'face to face'.

Because I think that this is our only life, that this world is the only world we can have and that we are always inside language and our other sign-systems, I am bound to follow Thomas Hobbes in saying that the old dream of absolute visionary knowledge was a mistake. No, we are always in language, always in time, always in 'secondariness'. But I also maintain that it is possible for us to be supremely happy now, here and as we are. See also *Above Us Only Sky* (pp. 33ff.) and other entries on time and language, including **Solar ethics, etc.**

In addition, there is the further objection to the monkish-mystical dream of absolute, immediate and infinitive knowledge of God in eternity, namely that it is too abstract and exalted for us ordinary mortals who are social beings bounded by language and time. It has been called 'the flight of the alone to the Alone'. Ordinary people rightly regard love as the highest value and prefer the more social conception of Heaven as 'the City of God'. I add only that this latter goal should be sought here and now, in this life. See the entries on **Life** and on **Solar Living.**

Transcendent and transcendental. These two terms are often confused. I try to stick to Kant's use (or what ought to have been the great man's use: he's not quite consistent *himself*). 'Transcendent' means climbing or ascending over or across. What is transcendent over us altogether surpasses us; it belongs to a higher level of being and exceeds the categories of our ordinary understanding. So the *transcendent* is the supremely great, out-there and 'other'.

What is 'transcendental' has to be sought in exactly the opposite direction, by a retrogressive kind of analysis. We work backwards, trying to discover what is always presupposed in our own thinking. In the Middle Ages, it was held that all true affirmative judgements about matters of fact presuppose five transcendentals, namely *Ens, Res, Unum, Verum, Bonum* (Be-ing, thinghood, unity, truth and goodness). Kant provides a vastly more sophisticated analysis backwards, which starts by asking, How do we get our ideas of space and time? We don't actually perceive either of them with our senses and must conclude that they are an *a priori* framework, within which we locate our perceptions. It's a necessary first step in the work of building a spatio-temporal world out of the disorderly tumult of our experience.

In summary, the Transcendent is what altogether surpasses us. It is 'metaphysical' or 'supernatural' – *both* words meaning 'beyond or above the natural'. The transcendental is what we must always presuppose. I don't see how we could ever have sufficient reason to believe that anything transcendent exists: maybe the very word is a philosophical mistake. What is transcendental is, I believe, mostly just language (in a broad sense), which we are always inside and which is the medium in which we think – even when praying. See also **Outsidelessness, Be-ing**, etc.

Truth. In the old pre-modern scheme of thought it was believed that because the divine Wisdom (or Logos, or Spirit) pervaded the whole created world; and because our minds are finite counterparts of the divine Mind, *therefore* Truth exists out-there and we are specially designed to be able to receive it, for example by the illumination of our minds from above, or by special inspiration – also from above.

This ancient idea of an objective Truth out there which comes down to us from above still pervades Christian and other religious language. But since around 1600 or so, there has been a progressively accelerating growth of purely man-made secular knowledge. It has grown so huge that it has overwhelmed and wiped out the earlier ideas of truth and knowledge.

To put the new position very shortly, we have gradually developed our own human ways to truth in the law courts, in history, in natural science and so on. Evidence, both primary and corroborating, is gathered and checked; hypotheses are put forward and tested and truth is always no more than the current consensus amongst those most active and best regarded in that subject-area – a consensus which will probably shift over time, so that all our knowledge is fallible. Paradoxically and interestingly, this new way to knowledge by critical testing and open debate produces only fallible truths. But it is now enormously more powerful than the old way to knowledge by receiving it from a higher, indeed a supreme, religious Authority. Undoubtedly, we must accept the newer account of knowledge: and I have therefore over the years gradually shed the last vestiges of belief in Revelation and belief in Tradition. Which is why, in recent works such as *The Fountain* (2010), I cannot go beyond what used to be called 'natural religion'.

An interesting corollary of all this is that Truth, like so much else, has been **democratized**. Not only is there no final **Answer**, no magic formula and no One great Author/Authority from Whom all truth comes, but the very idea of a true account of reality as a whole has faded. Most realists settle for some kind of 'approximationism', as I call it, the belief that over time science can and does achieve a progressively closer approximation to objective truth. But I oppose even that. All we can ever achieve is *enough to go on, for now*. Remember, on my view language does not and cannot *copy* reality and we shouldn't cling to the idea that one day we will succeed in making it do so. So on my view we can continue refining our theories in physics until we decide that it is no longer profitable to do so. In the short run and in the long run, our knowledge and our interest is practical. See also **Everything is a period piece.**

V

The Valuation of Life. An idea introduced in *The New Christian Ethics* (1988). As our language shows, in recent years we have largely given up the idea that values are natural and objective. Instead of talking about 'natural' rights and values, we now talk about *human* rights and values. Indeed, examination of our language soon makes it clear that most of the things we say carry or suggest valuations. A famous example of this is the remarkable list of derogatory words for women which Germaine Greer appended to *The Female Eunuch* in the 1960s. Some words interestingly carry conflicting valuations, for example when 'dog' suggests not only 'man's best friend' and 'faithful hound', but also 'dirty dog' and 'cur'. After the 1960s many 'liberation' movements understood that in order to improve their moral standing in society, they must campaign for changes in language, so that the public would be persuaded to give up derogatory words and phrases. In the event, homosexual people (relabelled 'gay'), black people and women have all successfully changed (or have largely changed) the language used about themselves in public.

Against this background, I argued that in Christian Ethics we should so speak and act as to achieve as high an overall valuation of everything in the lifeworld as is consistently possible. We should make a start by giving up derogatory usages about anybody.

This idea was a forerunner of my more recent attempt to argue that we should, in **solar living**, live entirely without **ressentiment**.

We are in the Void and we make the lot, the Discipline of the Void, Make a friend of the Void. It may be hard to believe of me nowadays, but I was once – during the winter of 1952–3 – an Evangelical convert. I had a strong feeling of warmth and of umbilical connection with God. When – as was inevitable – my naively **realistic** faith faded, I felt the horror of the Void (*horror vacui*). I felt like a spaceman, out for a 'walk' to do a repair job, whose lifeline back to the mother-ship is accidentally ruptured. He feels himself floating off into an infinite Void, alone, left out.

Mass loss of the old kind of theistic faith has been going on slowly for at least a century and a half in our society, and it has been traumatic for many people. Perhaps the most intense evocations of it, and of horror at the prospect of one's own death, are to be found in the poems of Thomas Hardy and in 'Aubade' (1977), Philip Larkin's last great poem.

This horror of being lost, shut out, excluded for ever, seems to be rather strongly Christian. Consider how intensely *crowded* representations of Heaven in Christian art usually are. Only a few mystics, such as Saint John of the Cross, love the way of *nada*, nothingness, or speak of 'the flight of the alone to the Alone'.

However, I was encouraged when young by the movement towards plain black paintings in the New York school of painting and began trying to learn to love the void. Think of the strand in empiricist philosophy which reached the conclusion that there is nothing beyond the veil of sense-experience; of the strand in Wittgenstein that thinks there is nothing beyond culture; and of the strand in Derrida that thinks there is nothing beyond 'the text'. I gradually began to practise the discipline of the Void as I became familiar with the way it is approached, over and over again, in philosophy. But my own versions of the Void – **anthropomonism, outsidelessness,** etc. –

are not intended to terrify. Philip Larkin seems to want us to *share* his utter, paralysing horror. I don't. I want to suggest that we learn a kind of Buddhist levity, lightness. It is part of **solar living**. See also **Emptiness**.

W

World. In English we have a history of using this word to mean Cosmos, that is, the realm of Nature out-there, considered as distinct from and prior to ourselves. An alternative popular term nowadays is 'the Universe'. However, it is very important to me that the word 'world' etymologically means the human world, the social world, 'the times' or 'the age' (Greek, *aion*) that we live in. It is important to me to argue that the primary world that we live in is the world in which ordinary natural language is completely at home, namely the world of our everyday life. Around this rather small nucleus there have developed since about the time of Shakespeare a great number of specialist extensions – notably the whole range of subjects studied in a modern university. But still, we all began in the ordinary human lifeworld: it was given to us with our mother-tongue, and we always presuppose it. We cannot entirely **transcend** it.

A corollary of this is that we must not forget that both scientific and religious thinking always presuppose the human lifeworld. Science should not pretend to absolute or 'dogmatic' truth, nor should religious belief: both are human and cultural activities. In science the observer is human, and the performance of experiments in laboratories always presupposes the human lifeworld. So theories are not checked against *nothing*: they are tested for their coherence with the way of things in the human lifeworld. Not even in modern physics can we attain absolute knowledge, for there can be no such thing.

Y

Saying Yes to life. By looking longingly up to Heaven, where they thought Jesus was enthroned until the hour of his return to earth, the earliest Christians gave to the new faith what became a permanently otherworldly orientation. This world and this life were downgraded in comparison with the glories of the world above. Even in the seventeenth century, when modern science was getting under way and human eyes were increasingly focused upon this world, the English *Book of Common Prayer* (1662) still has a Burial rite in which God is thanked for delivering 'this our *brother* (or sister) out of the miseries of this sinful world' and freeing *him* from 'the burden of the flesh'.

Friedrich Nietzsche was surely correct in saying that the received Church-version of Christianity was anti-life. There is no point in talking down and trying to escape from the only life we'll ever have. On the contrary, it is rational to say Yes to life, to value it highly and to believe that, with sufficient effort and hard work, we can make life much better for most people than it is. Even stronger, we should strive if we can to say Yes to life right up to the moment of our death.

Good examples of people early affected by Nietzsche's insistence on saying Yes to life include D. H. Lawrence and Albert Schweitzer. Note that ascetical, anti-life religion and philosophy tend to bear down particularly heavily upon women. In all three 'Abrahamic' faiths neo-conservative men measure their own religious seriousness by the degree to which they distance themselves from women.

Z

Zoe. Around the turn of the Millennium I was putting forward the view that the real religious achievement of the Modern period has been 'the sacralization of life'. The process of secularization was bringing long-established supernatural beings, goals and values back down to earth, and so leading to a steadily rising valuation of our ordinary everyday 'common' life.

This observation goes back to the late Middle Ages, when lay people in the towns first began to protest against the Church's teaching that virginity was superior to marriage, and that holy solitude was morally superior to family life. Now in the Modern period the sacralization of ordinary life has been taken so far as to become highly conspicuous in the idioms in ordinary language in which we speak of life.

But what is life? Sacralizing biological life soon leads to vitalism, which is objectionable as being scientific heresy, and because it may lead in the direction of social Darwinism and far right-wing politics. So I have generally maintained that by 'life' I mean chiefly the going-on of things in the human world, the world of our secular, human life: in short, the world of ordinary language, the so-called 'real world' of ordinary people.

In Greek there is a (rough) distinction between *bios*, which is commonly used to refer to *biological* life, and *zoe*, which refers especially to *human* life, its span, its activities and so on. The 'eternal life' of which the Gospel of John speaks is a supernaturally enhanced form of human life, 'the life of the world to come', lived in an eternal Today. Saint John's use of the word 'life' has been very influential: the Gospel uses it 36 times, plus the word 'living' 16 times, and the Greek word is always *zoe*. In the theological tradition ever since, life is *zoe*, which in effect distinguishes it clearly from *bios*.

The distinction is not always clear in the texts, but it is worth dwelling on the point today, because of the influence of Nietzsche. He wanted to secularize the concept of life dramatically, but in the process it is only too easy to bring the holy down to the merely healthy, and religious life down into mere pride in one's own animal vitality. Notice how careful the Buddhists are on this point: they encourage us to feel with and for 'all sentient beings' – 'all fellow-creatures', a Christian might say – but they never go near the testosterone-fuelled aggressiveness of bull males and 'strong Leaders'.

The Books

With some justice, I have been criticized for writing many more books than even the most devoted fan could be expected to read. Here is the record, and it is indeed about 'as long as your arm'. Places of publication are London, unless otherwise stated. Fuller bibliographies are readily available in various places: start with my website http://www.doncupitt. com/doncupitt.html

Christ and the Hiddenness of God, Lutterworth, 1971, reissued SCM Press, 1985.
Crisis of Moral Authority, Lutterworth, 1972, reissued SCM Press, 1985.
The Leap of Reason, SPCK Sheldon Press, 1976, reissued SCM Press, 1985.
The Worlds of Science and Religion, SPCK, 1976.
Who was Jesus? (with Peter Armstrong), BBC, 1977.
Explorations in Theology, SCM Press, 1979.
The Nature of Man, SPCK, 1979.
The Debate about Christ, SCM Press, 1979.
Jesus and the Gospel of God, Lutterworth, 1979.
Taking Leave of God, SCM Press, 1980 and many reissues.
The World to Come, SCM Press, 1982.
The Sea of Faith, BBC, 1984, revised editions SCM Press, 1994, 2003.
Only Human, SCM Press, 1985.
Life Lines, SCM Press, 1986.
The Long Legged Fly, SCM Press, 1987.
The New Christian Ethics, SCM Press, 1988.
Radicals and the Future of the Church, SCM Press, 1989.
Creation out of Nothing, SCM Press, 1990, with simultaneous US edition.

What is a Story?, SCM Press, 1991, reprint 1995.

The Time Being, SCM Press, 1992.

After All, SCM Press, 1994.

The Last Philosophy, SCM Press, 1995.

Solar Ethics, SCM Press, 1995, reissued 2005.

After God, New York: HarperCollins, Basic Books and London: Weidenfeld and Nicholson, 1997.

Mysticism After Modernity, Oxford: Basil Blackwell, 1997.

The Religion of Being, SCM Press, 1998.

The Revelation of Being, SCM Press, 1998.

The New Religion of Life in Everyday Speech, SCM Press, 1999.

The Meaning of It All in Everyday Speech, SCM Press, 1999.

Kingdom Come in Everyday Speech, SCM Press, 2000.

Philosophy's Own Religion, SCM Press, 2000.

Reforming Christianity, Santa Rosa, CA: Polebridge Press, 2001.

Emptiness and Brightness, Santa Rosa, CA: Polebridge Press, 2001.

Is Nothing Sacred? Essays in Non-Realist Philosophy of Religion, New York: Fordham University Press, 2002.

Life, Life, Santa Rosa, CA: Polebridge Press, 2003.

The Way to Happiness, Santa Rosa, CA: Polebridge Press, 2005.

The Great Questions of Life, Santa Rosa, CA: Polebridge Press, 2006.

The Old Creed and the New, SCM Press, 2006.

Radical Theology, Santa Rosa, CA: Polebridge Press, 2006.

Impossible Loves, Santa Rosa, CA: Polebridge Press, 2007.

Above Us Only Sky, Santa Rosa, CA: Polebridge Press, 2008.

The Meaning of the West, SCM Press, 2008.

A New Method of Religious Enquiry, Beijing: Religion and Culture Publishing House, 2008 (Chinese only).

Jesus and Philosophy, SCM Press, 2009.

Theology's Strange Return, SCM Press, 2010.

A New Great Story, Salem, OR: Polebridge Press, 2010.

The Fountain: A Secular Theology, SCM Press, 2010.

Turns of Phrase, SCM Press, 2011.